STORIES OF SURVIVAL

Conversations with Native North Americans

Edited by Remmelt and Kathleen Hummelen

ISBN 0-377-00150-3
Editorial Offices: 475 Riverside Drive, Room 772, New York, NY 10115
Distribution Offices: P.O. Box 37844, Cincinnati, OH 45237
Copyright © 1985 Friendship Press, Inc.
Printed in the United States of America

CONTENTS

PREFACE

The pizza was gone and the conversation was ending when Sherman leaned heavily over the table and said, "It's survival. That's what it's all about, survival." In that instant we both knew that, in fact, survival is what this book is about:

Surviving the wars.

Surviving the government.

Surviving cultural genocide

Surving as a person when told, "You're not an Indian. There are no Indians left!"

These are stories about survival. Each of the speakers has survived both as a person and as a member of a larger community. Educator, activist, artist, spiritual leader—each is working to ensure the survival of their people. And each is equally important to this challenge.

Our mandate was to develop individual profiles dealing with issues affecting Native people and Native communities in Canada and the United States. We were somewhat apprehensive about this format for two reasons. First, because such personal stories might lead readers to see the issues in individual terms rather than encourage their social analysis. Second, Native people are more likely to see themselves as members of communities rather than as individuals; the individual profile format might then be inconsistent with "the message" as they perceive it to be. Nevertheless, many people have been willing to open their lives to us and it has been a privilege to listen to them.

The profiles were compiled from taped interviews conducted in person or by telephone. The words and conversational tone are those of the person interviewed with editorial changes only for the sake of clarity.

For the non-Native reader, two imperatives emerge: repentance and listening. Repentance requires an emotional, spiritual and intellectual recognition of the enormous injustice the dominant culture has perpetrated on Native people. It means recognizing the depths of our individual and corporate racism. Such repentance is not likely to happen overnight; we have a lot to undo and unlearn.

Listening means opening ourselves to the voices in these pages as they speak out in anger, frustration, determination and celebration. As the reader listens, she or he may respond with the same emotions. Our hope is that these stories of survival will inspire all of us to further the dialogue and continue, as Vine Deloria says, "to translate ideas back and forth."

Remmelt and Kathleen Hummelen

Tepee in Wisconsin used in ceremonies of the Native American Church.

"I LIKE TO SHOW THE BEAUTY IN LIFE."

Allen Angeconeb

I come from an Ojibway reserve called Lac Seul up in northwestern Ontario. I was the sixth of nine children, four girls and five boys. My father hunted and trapped in the winter months and in the summer he fished for freshwater fish while we children were sent to pick berries. When I was six my parents sent me to a boarding school near Sioux Lookout. That's where I learned my English.

From the time I was four or five I drew on my mother's walls. I made drawings from traditional Ojibway myths. When I was about thirteen, an art teacher took an active interest in my work. The same year, an older brother who was studying graphic design introduced me to oil paints, acrylics, pastels, colored pencils, different types of paper and canvas. The next year I read a book by the first Woodland artist, Norval Morrisseau. I was already interested in doing visual interpretations of the Ojibway culture and this gave me an extra boost. When I was seventeen I had my first exhibition and since then I have exhibited regularly with other artists, even once with Morrisseau himself.

In 1975 I joined Canada World Youth/Jeunesse Canada Mondiale, an organization that sends young Canadians to developing countries so they will become more aware of themselves and Canada and the world as a whole. I went to Malaysia and became

Allen Angeconeb is an artist from Lac Seul, Ontario.

intrigued by the designs and motifs of the different cultures and religions. I was particularly facinated by the sculptures that are done by Malaysia's so-called aboriginal people, the Orung Aslie. They work in mahogany and their sculptural forms, often of their gods, are very free—quite different from the Malay, Chinese and East Indian art forms. This society is still very basic; many Orung Aslie live in rural areas of Malaysia where the Malay government has given them so-called reserves with free education. I came away feeling that the Orung Aslie are not very impressed with Malay culture or with Western culture in general. This was one parallel between the Orung Aslie culture and my own Ojibway culture. But there were others—hunting, for example. In both cultures, this is a very sacred act and there are certain rituals that a hunter must follow in order for himself and the animals and his environment to survive. I felt that my own background was reinforced by the Orung Aslie culture.

In the last few years I have become intrigued with the idea of a universal art form. In the painting I did for the cover of this book I was trying to capture this idea while still maintaining a North American style. The circle in the center of the painting represents North America. I have heard that North America is considered more or less a world in itself, so the four points of the circle represent the four corners of North America. This circle is set inside a bigger circle with lines coming out of it. This circle represents the earth. The four colors of races are shown in the four corners of this circle: to the north is the white race, to the east is the yellow race, to the south is the red race and to the west is the black race. The smaller circle of North America is red, signifying the red race.

There are four human figures on the four points of the design. These figures standing with their hands in the air represent a universal motif that is found in the art of many so-called primitive societies; similar designs have been discovered in France, Spain, Northern Africa and South America. The figures' hands are quite large in proportion to the body, the palms facing out. The legs are bent and the feet go sideways so you can see the length of the foot. There is a prominent line down the chest of each figure with other lines coming out from it. This linework may be a very simplified design of the anatomy. I believe it is also a universal motif, since it's found in Australian Aboriginal art and in some of the designs that were done by Inuit peoples prior to the arrival of the Europeans. It looks like the lines inside a leaf, but where the design comes from, I don't know. The figure's head is a very crude rectangle. This, too, is taken from a universal motif. The triangular eyes are borrowed from those of the dolls made by Hopi Indians. On top of the head are feathers, eagle feathers, which are prominent in many North American Indian cultures.

In the Woodland art form as it was developed by Norval Morrisseau there are several things that are distinctive. One is the use of black, which makes a very bold design. Woodland art sometimes looks like an X-ray or a very crude interpretation of the anatomy—vertebrae, heart, etc. Sometimes you'll see the "external anatomy" as well—feather patterns, fur, even scales. There is also a strong spiritual dimension to Woodland art, and the idea of taking some elements of mythology and interpreting them visually. But recently there has been a shift away from representing spiritual ideas, towards showing things that are more ordinary and everyday.

Not all my work is in this form, though. I have done a few pieces that could be called social statements. One I did back in 1980 is called "Technical Mythology". One day I was sitting in a small house in rural Quebec thinking of the modern-day mythology of the so-called civilized urban world. I thought of the mythologies of Ojibway and other traditional societies and I remembered one Ojibway legend I had heard in my youth— the legend of the loon and the grebe. In this legend there were two personalities. The loon was very kind and friendly, but the grebe was selfish and rude. When I did this particular design of the loon and the grebe I showed both of them in rectangles— very rigid, not very fluid. Western philosophy and rationalism seem to be in very neat patterns like this and the rigid rectangles illustrate the idea. The interior of the loon and the grebe are white, but everything else is outlined in black. The background of the painting is in yellow, red and blue, the three primary colors. These colors are also very rigid, flat and cold. They have no personality or warmth; they are just there. This is how I see modern "mythology" as compared to a traditional, living mythology. A friend told me the painting was ugly. I said, "Thank you. That's a compliment. That's what it's supposed to be."

The painting may be a social statement, but it's not political. I've never wanted to get politically involved. I want to show the beauty of life instead of being negative, lashing out. It's not escapism—it's what I like to do. If someone else wants to make physical or angry statements, that's for them to do.

When I visit my parents I like to spend a month or so to actually "feel" the place again, get re-energized by Ojibway culture, ideas and philosophy.

I cross-country ski, spend time in the woods, go ice-fishing with my father, trap and hunt with my brothers. Sometimes I go out on the trapline and meditate.

I speak Ojibway with my parents. With my brothers and sisters, it's fifty-fifty English and Ojibway. When I'm by myself or I'm the only Ojibway around I take time out to think in Ojibway. I want to maintain my language and the Ojibway way of thinking. When I paint, I mostly think in English, but many of my ideas are very Ojibway.

One of the things I enjoy most when I go back is seeing the old people who sometimes talk about traditional ideas and things that are in some ways sacred. I do enjoy going back and maintaining the same outlook as the traditional people, the elders. And I think they are glad to see that I have kept that.

"WHEN I WAS IN SCHOOL, HISTORY BEGAN WITH COLUMBUS!"

Paulette Fairbanks

I grew up on the White Earth Reservation in northern Minnesota. It's an Ojibway reservation, approximately thirty-six square miles of land located in three different counties. It's known as a "checkerboard" reservation: some of the land is state-owned, some county-owned, some Indian-owned. The community where I grew up is called Pine Point, located in Becker County.

My father was a logger and trapper and he spent a lot of time every spring out trapping beaver. He used to trap mink before there were so many mink farms and once in a while he would trap otter. In the fall he harvested wild rice like a lot of other Ojibway people. The community is traditional in the sense that a lot of these activities still go on.

I went to an all-Indian school on the reservation for seven years and then to a predominantly white high school. Indian students were the only minority. It was a totally new environment for us. Before, our school had been all-Indian. Our parents, the community and all our friends had been Indian. We were all pretty much in the same social class and no one thought much about things like income-level because there wasn't a whole lot of difference between us—except that maybe people who worked in the school or the church had a more stable income.

Starting high school was an experience in culture shock. The Indian students encountered non-Indian students for the first time and *we* were the outsiders. Definitely the outsiders. We were bussed in and bussed out so we never became involved with extracurricular activities. There were exceptions to that, a few students who stayed for basketball or football or whatever, but very few because it was so hard for them to arrange transportation. We all felt alienated from everything going on in that school, and I know this was not my feeling alone because so many Indian students dropped out. When I was in high school, the dropout rate was 80 to 90 percent among Indians.

These high school experiences are of tremendous importance to me because I know that everything I am doing as an adult goes back to my development as a young person in that environment. Who I react to positively and who I back away from today comes from years of conditioning and growing up with

Paulette Fairbanks is an education consultant with various Native organizations. She lives in New York City.

racism. Many towns bordering reservations have people with negative attitudes towards Indian people. The bigotry comes out in different ways. For example, in the town where I attended high school there were certain hangouts where Indian people just did not go. There weren't any signs, people just knew. I also remember the feeling of separateness—for example, the bus we rode was yellow like the others, yet the teachers would refer to it as the "Indian bus."

A lot of subtle things added up to our knowing we were not accepted. The students who dropped out knew they weren't wanted. Those Indian students who graduated, like me, were held up as shining stars for other poor kids trying to struggle through. I often wonder if those who left early were the smarter ones, whether they were less damaged than those of us who stayed. I think I must carry around a lot of psychological scars. Being with people who don't want you around is bound to rub off on you in some way.

The tremendous waste of Indian potential in our educational system is one of my main concerns. I don't think non-Indians view it that way, though! I know people who have a tremendous amount of talent who have low opinions of themselves because their gifts are not recognized by non-Indians. That's one of the horrors of what's happened with the educational system and until it's reversed in some way, both communities will end up losing. Talented Indian people will drift from day to day without the skills to get decent employment and non-Indian society will lose by having people they don't know what to do with.

Of course, educational systems vary. Some Indian people live on reservations or in rural non-reservation settings; some live in cities. You find one extreme or the other and everything in between. And Indian people vary tremendously, too: some groups have retained their language, history and culture and some groups have gone through centuries of conditioning to make them forget it all.

The teachers vary, too. Some I have met have made a real effort to learn about their students and to be well-informed, good teachers. But for the most part I find that teachers' attitudes are pretty appalling. They have very limited information about Indian people and the sad part is that the children they teach pick up the same limited knowledge. It's a constant struggle to counteract these experiences. Many Indian people find that they become instructors to every non-Indian they encounter!

When I was first in elementary school the students were Indian but all the teachers were white. Later, one of the Indian students I knew graduated from college and returned as director of the school we had attended as children. Around that time there was an effort to close the school, which would have meant all the young children would have to be bussed to a white school. This director led the community's struggle to keep the school; he managed to get "experimental" status for it. Then he introduced Indian culture and history into the curriculum and hired a number of Indian teachers. When I was growing up there wasn't anything in the curriculum to differentiate our school from any other public school in Minnesota.

I think that teachers and parents *can* become informed. They can react if they see negative stereotyping of Indians on television programs, especially children's programs. The mass media perpetuates a lot of the negative stereotypes, too. For example, you'll see an article about Indian people having a meeting and instead of specifying which group, the headline will say, "Indians had a big pow-wow." Journalists should cover events like these seriously instead of using stereotyped, cutesy language.

Some Indian groups have produced evaluative criteria that provide good guidelines for recognizing stereotypes, because even everyday things like greeting cards tend to show negative stereotypes if they portray Indians at all. Teachers should hold workshops to learn how to use these criteria. Another thing schools can do is find out about Indian-produced teaching materials. A lot of Indian people are now working on histories that portray Indian people the way *we* think we should be portrayed. Most of this material is not produced through mainstream

publishers and this is one more area where we should try to make inroads.

History, when I was in school, began with Columbus. If Indians were mentioned at all it was in a paragraph or two, and they were so far removed from my existence that they were unrecognizable. Ever since European contact our history has been one of a dominant society trivializing our language, culture and history with an attitude of cultural superiority. For example, comments about our religion make it out to be all superstition. Imagine that sort of attitude about another major world religion!

The Indian world view actually involves an attitude of respect for and equality with all of life, including plants, animals and other human beings. I always like the fact that one of our strong symbols is a circle, as opposed to the hierarchical pyramid where you have some people who are higher up than others. We all have something to contribute equally—that's an important way of thinking if you are concerned to prevent the destruction of the earth.

Our collective memory goes back so long. And that includes our knowledge of the earth and the universe. I don't think anyone ever sat down and said to me, "This is an Indian value." You sort of grow up with things and later in life, when you have encountered other people, you can analyze who *you* are. One of the main values I was taught was generosity. Whenever anyone came to visit my grandparents provided food for them—it was just the thing to do. If you didn't offer food you were violating some kind of unwritten rule. People in my community would become angry if they thought someone was becoming stingy or aquisitive. And since it was a small community, people were really involved with each other. Whenever someone died there would be a wake and my grandparents or some of the older people would get together and sing hymns in Ojibway, take food to the bereaved family and just be available to comfort them.

My parents and grandparents were very important to me and my brothers and sisters because they were loving, good people. My grandparents were together over sixty years—that's practically unheard of today! They spoke Ojibway and English, but their first language was Ojibway. My mother is fluent in the language too. In fact, I remember she used to translate for Ojibway people at the clinic when they had to communicate with non-Indians. At home, she pretty much used English. My father knows the language too, but not as well as my mother, so English was the predominant language in our household.

There have been a lot of changes over the years. As the younger generation grew up a lot of them left. When I was growing up, nearly everybody lived in their own little house separated from the other houses. Then the government put up cluster housing projects and it was as if urban housing had been put in the middle of an Indian reservation. A lot of people didn't like it. They liked having their own yard and their own piece of land and their own sense of belonging. If you live in a housing project that's not really yours there's a temporary, institutional kind of feeling.

Right now I'm working on a doctorate in educational administration at the University of Minnesota; I worked in education for a number of years in Minnesota. I attended the Harvard Graduate School of Education for a year and then came to New York, where I've lived for nearly three years. I have also been working as a consultant to the Boston Indian Council on an Indian adult education program called Project Advance.

My life has changed considerably since I've been in the East. Before, I was living in an area with a large Indian population and working in one institution, the Minneapolis public schools. Now I'm doing a variety of things in an entirely different environment.

This design, and those on pages 12, 16, 20, 24, 44, 48, 52, 58, and 66 are taken from Decorative Art of the Southwestern Indians, *New York: Dover Publications, Inc. 1961.*

"ESSENTIALLY, AMERICAN INDIANS ARE CAPTIVE NATIONS."

Matthew Snipp

Probably the best way to describe me is to say I'm a transplanted Okie. All of my family are from Oklahoma. My mother is Choctaw and my father is Cherokee. They both moved out to California after the war so my dad could work on the oil fields. Now all my folks have moved back to Oklahoma; no oil in California.

I did undergraduate work at the University of California at Davis. That's when I became politically involved with American Indians. For a couple of years I was deeply involved with something called DQ University, an Indian/Chicano alternative college. It was supposed to be a collective effort between Indians and Chicanos in California, a strange political alliance that served everybody's purpose at the time. After I finished up at Davis I got my master's and PhD in sociology from the University of Wisconsin. While I was there I worked with urban Indian groups and with some Winnebago and Chippewa tribes. Then I took my first academic job at the University of Maryland.

In the U.S.A. there are a fraction under 1.6 million Indians. They are scattered, with forty-nine percent living in what the census defines as "metropolitan" areas and about fifty-one percent living in "rural" areas. Out of this fifty-one percent, the majority live on what are called reservations or on "tribal trust" land. "Tribal trust" is a legal term for a parcel of land near a reservation that isn't actually part of it.

Matthew Snipp is Professor of Sociology at the University of Maryland.

There are, as a rough guess, over three hundred tribes that are recognized by the Bureau of Indian Affairs (BIA). One thing that is overlooked by many people is that some Indian tribes are not recognized by the federal government. There *is* a process through which tribes can become recognized, though; in the last few years the Kickapoo tribe in Texas and the Biloxi tribe in Louisiana have actually petitioned to be recognized. There's a difference, you see: unrecognized tribes never went to war against the federal government. They were small tribes that sort of fell between the cracks and never had a treaty with the government to document their existence. Other tribes never organized themselves enough to become recognized. The Wisconsin Winnebago were not recognized until the early 1960's because in theory, all the Winnebago had been moved from Wisconsin to a reservation in Nebraska. So when we use figures like "three hundred" Indian tribes we're really talking about tribes that are recognized by the U.S. government.

Another important thing to remember is that Indian tribes are considered sovereign nations. This sovereignty was established through the battles of the late 1800's. Sovereign tribal authorities were engaging the United States in military actions and the U.S. government recognized this fact. Ever since then, sovereignty and recognition of the tribes and their land base in the United States has occurred through the treaty process.

Something like 370 treaties were signed between 1790 and 1870. Then in 1871, an appropriation act forbade Congress, the President or anyone else to engage in further treaties with American Indian tribes. It seems they were no longer much of an issue.

In the early 1890's came the allotment acts. Senator Henry Dot, who passed the main allotment act, professed to be interested in the well-being of Indians. His way of dealing with the poverty and disease on reservations was to get Indians off reservations. The idea was that reservations were places where Indians practised traditional values and lifestyles as hunters and fishermen and that if this was their only way of surviving, it wasn't working. So allotment acts were designed to parcel out reservation land. They were administered by the Bureau of Indian Affairs. Agents would be sent out to talk to Indian people; if the Indians signed up, they terminated all further claims of tribal membership and the federal government extended United States citizenship to them. The idea was that Indians would become small farmers and eventually be assimilated into the culture and disappear. From 1880 until about

1920, a massive amount of Indian land that had been set aside in treaties was allotted this way. At that time, the vision of America was tied up with manifest destiny, the melting pot, the idea that everybody should be Americanized.

The extent to which Indians have been ignored by the government has varied a great deal throughout U.S. history. I would say that policy towards Indians has been divided between two major influences: that of Henry Jackson and that of John Marshall. In the early 1800's, the old Indian fighter Henry Jackson pushed for the Indian Removal Act which would have moved all the tribes west of the Appalachian Mountains. He was essentially trying to use military force to annihilate Indian tribes. In Jackson's world view there was no place for American Indians on the continent.

To counteract this attitude was the reaffirmation of tribal sovereignty pronounced by Chief Justice John Marshall. In a series of landmark decisions which have shaped Indian policy to this day, Marshall affirmed the principle that tribes are indeed sovereign in a special way. He believed that the federal government needed to recognize tribal laws and policies and that tribes, as sovereign entities, have claims on the land and resources of this continent. The history of Indian policy has always been in tension between John Marshall's principles and Henry Jackson's attitude. Jackson wanted to wipe Indians out; Marshall said: No, you have to take care of them—or at least recognize that they have the right to exist.

In the late 1940's the Indian Claims Commission was established in the United States to look into treaty rights and other claims that tribes brought—for example, claims that the government did not pay for land it took. Most of the legal grounds for these claims are based on treaties. And most of them have been settled. But some have been contested. In the early 1970's, for example, a river tribe up in northern California received a settlement of forty-nine cents an acre for prime forest land. The Pit River Tribe had won their claim, but they had been given market value at the time that the land was taken! They were very unhappy about it and some people sent their checks back as a protest.

In the early 1950's a house concurrent resolution sought to terminate the federal government's responsibility towards American Indians; in other words, they wanted to legislate the Indians out of existence and terminate all the reservations. One reason was that there weren't enough jobs on the reservations. The Relocation Program of the 1950's

and 60's was designed to move people off reservations and bring them into cities, teach them how to work in factories, be welders, mechanics, essentially blue-collar workers. This was the federal government's response to unemployment: instead of trying to develop the reservations, they moved the people off with the hope that they would find jobs and asssimilate themselves into urban life. Some reservations *were* terminated, in fact, but it didn't get very far because from that time onward there was increasing awareness that American Indians really are a distinct people and they are not simply going to assimilate into American society and disappear.

Throughout the 1960's, amidst all the poverty legislation that Kennedy and Johnson began, special measures were included for Indian reservations. In 1973, the Nixon administration was responsible for advocating the Indian Self-Determination Act, a push for greater tribal self-determination. What Reagan knows about Indians was probably learned from his experience in Hollywood. I think the prevailing view in Washington today is that programs for Indians are as useless and unnecessary as programs for anyone else.

American Indians have gone from being fully sovereign nations to a kind of status that I call "captive nations." This means that the government recognizes the sovereign status of American Indians along with the fact that they have been militarily defeated.

On many reservations, the primary source of employment is either the Bureau of Indian Affairs or the tribal government. Tribal governments rely on federal monies or public programs for the majority of what they get. Today, as a result of the cuts in federal expenditures, unemployment has soared. One Navajo reservation went from an unemployment rate of fifteen percent to about fifty percent, largely because of cuts in federal programs. So we are talking about a really major impact.

Today, the trend of more and more Indians moving to cities seems to have reached a plateau. There is still a lot of "circular migration"—that is, Indians moving off the reservation for a short period of time to go and work in a city and make money, then spending the winter at home. The problem is that Indians who live in cities no longer have the umbrella of the tribal government to protect them; they are on their own. And programs for urban Indians have also shrunk under the current administration.

For reservation Indians today, the Bureau of Indian Affairs is like Big Brother. You can't turn around without running into it in some way. You can't lease your land or add improvements without getting the

BIA's approval. And if you do lease your land, you don't ever see the check—you see a BIA check, because the agency is responsible for collecting the money and dispersing it. All this is a pervasive fact of life.

I think one thing people need to be sensitive to is that ''American Indians'' are not a single ''ethnic group.'' American Indian tribes are as diverse as European nations. People should also be sensitive to the fact that Indians have a form of social organization that is every bit as legitimate as that of a county or state government.

I'm expecting more pressure from the government towards assimilation and acculturation in the coming years. With its enormous federal deficit I think the government is going to continue to try to get out of its responsibility to people, and Indians are not going to be exempt from this. I detect a very nasty mood, very little tolerance, understanding or willingness to accept differences. But Indians have a center of strength that will keep them together. They will get through.

This child's drawing, and those on pages 11, 14, 23, 38, 51, 54 and 70 were taken from Everybody Likes Ducks, *a book of stories, poems and illustrations by students at the S.T.E.P. (Short Term Emergency Placement) Home in Kenora, Ontario. Copyright 1984 by Gregory H. Sparks.*

"THE TRADITIONAL WESTERN ANSWERS OFFER NO SOLUTION TO ME."

Vine Deloria

I am from the Sioux tribe and grew up in western South Dakota on the Pine Ridge Reservation. I was raised in a border town where the majority were mixed-blood Indians. Whites have moved in during the last fifty years; in fact, in think the town is now predominantly white.

My father and grandfather were Episcopal clergymen. I went to a seminary and got a degree too, but I was never ordained. I never wanted to be part of any church. I also went to law school and got a law degree. Those two things seem so far away now, it's hard to remember.

When I was growing up, education was where you could get it. Looking back, I wish I'd had an opportunity to get a good undergraduate degree in history or literature, but when I grew up, just getting a degree was a novelty. Today I teach political science, education and courses on federal/Indian relations.

It's difficult, writing about all this within American society. Depending on the audience you want to address you may or may not be able to find a publisher because the publishing industry in the United States has a very fixed image of what Indians are—a romanticized and nonsensical image. My first book was a broadside against American society in general, an attempt to wake people up to the fact that there *are* Indians. Two years ago, I wrote a five hundred page book on what has happened to Indians since World War II. It was pretty realistic, and the publisher I had a contract with turned it down. They were expecting something more romanticized: Indians are very spiritual, Mother Earth and all that. They didn't really want to believe that most Indians drive cars and know what a telephone is. They got terribly upset: "No one wants to read this kind of thing." That had been my best effort—a realistic appraisal of who Indians are today and what their problems are and I found out that people didn't want to read about it. It's a tough situation.

I write primarily to give an emotional and intellectual boost to Indians' growth process. I do that by demonstrating that some of the ideas in Indian society have a more universal application than most Indians expect.

Vine Deloria is an author and a professor at the University of Arizona.

What I'm doing is trying to translate ideas back and forth. But the problem with whites is, they can't take a single idea and grow with it. Almost anything you tell them, their response is: "Isn't that nice; isn't that interesting." It just gets boring as hell when you're a minority spokesman and they invite you to a conference and expect you to say exactly the same thing you said at the last conference. Then you start to realize that this society is not making any intellectual progress at all. What they're doing is reciting the same slogans in different contexts. Things only *appear* new because they change the characters at the conference or the covers of the books. The more I think about it the more perplexed I am as to how you go about changing anything in this country. Nobody seems able to *reflect* on anything.

At different times of your life you have different questions. My question at the present time relates to institutions. Indians, by and large, don't formalize things. They work through customs. Whites, on the other hand, can hardly do anything without creating an organization, with staff, to do it. So my question is, assuming that every group of people were at a certain time in their history in a tribal state: What happened to certain groups that made them think they had to institutionalize and formalize everything? To Indians, individuals are granted dignity by participating. Dignity in white society seems to depend on what status you have. If you're a professor you have a certain status whether as a person you deserve it or not. So much human emotion is vested in institutions because they are what endow you with prestige.

I'm interested in this question today because there's tremendous pressure coming from the government to get Indians to set up institutions that look like the institutions in white society: courts, child adoption agencies, social welfare agencies. Setting these things up takes a lot of human emotion. And many Indians are resisting them more and more. The question should be directed to white society: Why do you feel you have to institutionalize something in order to experience it?

The struggle between any two groups of people who disagree comes when the minority continue to have confidence in themselves while facing overwhelming restraints set by the majority. If you don't identify that as the basis of the problem you've lost the ballgame.

The big fight out here is over water rights. The question among Indians is, should they appropriate as much water under the law as they presently get? Or should they go along with the government, which is urging everyone to see the present water shortage as an issue of the allocation of all the water in the West? The point is, Indians will have to commit themselves to *use* all the water they appropriate once the rights are determined. And this might mean committing themselves to a lot of water development they might not need or want. The struggle is always in specific terms like this: Do you want an airport or do you want a new school? There's always a "prize".

What's happened is that most of the parties in the struggle want to determine their own water rights because they feel they may lose something if they don't. This is the current doctrine of the minority: If we don't do it now, we'll never get the chance to do it. If you apply this to other areas of life, you've got to be crazy. I think that first you have to ask: What is it I really want to do and how do I plan to do it? What happens, though, is that the minority keep on falling in with the rhythms of the majority and that proves to be very destructive to their community.

In the United States most people tend to be politically irresponsible. They don't care what their senator or congressman does so long as it doesn't affect them. They don't even care what laws are on the books as long as they work to their advantage. They don't have an underlying sense of justice.

What responsibilities does the U.S. government have towards Indians? Remember that Indians started off as foreign nations existing outside the constitutional framework. Why should they have "constitutional rights" now, if they were outside the U.S. Constitution from the very beginning?

But the government does have a responsibility towards people whose society they engulfed. Of course responsibility like this requires a very vigorous moral posture and it's been my experience that in the United States the only thing anyone understands is force. The United States puts pressure on people in other countries to do what the United States wants. To me, that's total barbarianism. And Indians are caught in the middle of it. When the government tries to extend constitutional rights and protections to Indians it's only to the degree that Indians adopt the behavior patterns of the white man. And since that is unsatisfactory to most traditional Indians, there's your conflict.

It's a conflict with a society that has no tradition, no stability, where people move every three years and communities can't exist; where the big ceremonies are the Academy Awards and the Superbowl; where magazines create instant celebrities and can summarize a person's life and personality in a page and a half of glossy photos. It's a conflict with a society where you don't even find community in Christianity, in my opinion. You get fifteen hundred people in a sports arena: Do you all accept God? Yes? Okay,

fine. But none of those people know who each other is as a person or gives a damn about them. In a system like this, ultimately you can use another person as a source of replacement parts. We're so capitalistic that surveys were submitted at Congressional hearings saying it was perfectly permissible for the poor to sell organs to the rich. Our conflict is with a system where the majority of people are not only poor, but have very little help given to them to make them better off than they are.

Even the beliefs of the majority are presented in a dictatorial fashion to minority peoples: This is right and this is why we're superior. It may take minority people their whole lives to get inside this intellectual structure and see that not only *don't* white people know more, but they faked a lot of what they do know! So when I begin to ask fundamental questions the traditional Western answers offer no solution to me.

I think I lost faith in Western science before I lost faith in Western religion. The more I studied, the more I realized that a lot of it didn't make sense to me. I don't feel the need to describe human relationships—or the supernatural—in terms of a trial court, which to me is basically what Christian theology is. It boils down to this: Man is a sinner, he's condemned, he needs not only an advocate but someone to pay the penalty. If you believe in this scenario, you're saved.

I don't have any unpleasant memories of my religious background, but over the last ten years, whenever I have given a critique of western society or Christianity, people jump on me, saying: You're just trying to escape from your mission background! They attack me as a person rather than attacking my ideas, because the ideas are too incisive—they hit them in the gut.

I look at all my experiences simply as things that helped me find out who I was at a certain time in my life. For example, I was in the Marines for two years. Now, I don't go around parading in uniform, but I have some great memories of the Marines. If I were in the Marines today I think I'd go AWOL because I wouldn't want to kill people who don't deserve killing. Anyway, the reason I adopt peaceful stands today is *not* because I was once a Marine and I feel guilty about it! In the same way, I am not trying to escape the experience of growing up with Christianity—it's just hard for me to remember it. I don't think it has shaped very many of my present postures. But I do remember the good times when I was a kid.

"THE METIS ARE MANITOBA'S HERITAGE . . . WE TAKE PRIDE IN THE FACT THAT WE ARE A BLEND."

Sherry Theobald

I have lived in Manitoba most of my life, though we moved thirty-five times when I was a kid; my dad was in the armed forces.

I have degrees in music and education from the University of Manitoba. While I was in school I was a member of the Indian Metis Inuit Student Association. One summer I worked with the Manitoba Metis Federation on a project called the Metis Pride Project. I did a lot of research and wrote a number of stories, which they published. After I graduated, one of my professors, a Metis, asked if I would consider doing a program on the local cable TV channel for the Metis Federation. The idea was to break down stereotypes by interviewing Indian, Metis and Inuit people to find out their ideas and accomplishments and celebrate their lives. That was in 1973. In 1976 the program went over to a local channel and has been there ever since as a half-hour weekly show.

"Woodsmoke and Sweetgrass" is basically a talk show. I felt from the beginning that it would best serve Native people if it could be an open forum where peo-

Sherry Theobald is host of "Woodsmoke and Sweetgrass," the oldest and longest-running Native talk show on Canadian television. It is broadcast by CKY TV in Winnipeg, a CTV affiliate.

ple would feel comfortable being interviewed. Ten years ago, many of the people I interviewed had never appeared on TV before and some did not speak English as a first language, so they were uncomfortable and embarrassed at first. Today we have a variety of people on the show, from grandmothers, beadworkers and children to artists, business people and government employees. In my interviews I would never attack a person or argue with them. The whole point is to find out who the person is, talk to them about their interests and how they feel about specific topics.

The main issues people want to talk about today are land claims, education and health. Each one of these topics can cover a large area. Take health. In Manitoba, forty clean water systems have been installed by the Indian Affairs Department and according to the Director of Indian Affairs, not one of them works. Why don't they work? Apparently there are mechanical failures, they freeze up in the winter, they don't have anyone to maintain them. So clean water *is* a problem. I have had people on the program who talked about violent death. Others discussed neonatal death. That was a major problem ten years ago when the show started, when the number of baby deaths in our community made it resemble a third world country. The situation today is not terrific but it is much better than it was. Access to health care is another concern. In isolated areas it is very hard to get a plane when you need one. A lot of people live in Winnipeg because the city is the only place where they can get health care.

In the area of education, language issues are a high priority to some people; others talk about self-control of the schools. Residential schools were abolished a long time ago, but most children still have to leave their reserve to go to school. They end up in a Winnipeg school, living in a boarding house, which isn't much better than the residential schools. A lot of the kids who come to the city are older than the rest of the kids in their class. They are not especially unhappy, not beaten or anything, but at the same time they're far away from home and I think that is cruel and unusual punishment. In one family I know of, the mother did not want her children to be boarded anyplace so she moved to Winnipeg too, and now she and her children commute back and forth to the reserve.

At Brandon University there is a full program for training people and making them hirable. Even people with very little education can go through a course that makes them ready for technical training. There is another course at the University of Manitoba for Native students who want to be doctors or nurses.

If they qualify, they sign up and they can get special help to make sure they get through. So things are coming along a little—not enough, but a little. People want to feel that they are actually doing things rather than waiting for someone else to do things for them. That is why they want the economic base—to handle their health problems, their children's welfare, their education.

Metis has the same root word in French as it does in Spanish. Down by the southern border, a *Mestiso* is a mixed-blood person. If you are part Indian, Metis is the word that is *used*. They also use another word here—*Bois-brule;* it means burnt sticks.

The Hudson's Bay Company arrived in 1697 but it wasn't until 1809 that there was a white woman in Manitoba. A hundred years is a long time. A book I know called *Many Tender Ties,* really a beautiful book, discusses the intermarriage between white men and Indian women. There were so many mixed families that a new society emerged. Some of the wives eventually went to England with their husbands and some stayed here if the husband went back.

Many of the Metis people spoke Indian, French and English, so they tended to be the traders, the people who could go back and forth between cultures. They were the buffalo hunters; they ran the Red River carts. It was a Metis who designed the York boat, a Metis who invented isinglass.

My Indian family comes from the Southwest. As a matter of fact, my Indian name is WalkingStick. The name is Cherokee, but I'm a mixture of things—a real Heinz 57! A lot of women are that way. For instance, if you were a trapper's daughter you went to different places; your mother might have been Cree and your grandmother might have been Ojibway or Potawatamee or whatever. The Metis weren't a population that stayed put.

By 1850 or so, Manitoba had a regular population of people who were part Indian and part French, English or Scot, or inter-mixed. You couldn't say this person is this much Indian or belongs to such-and-such a tribe. But all these people were very much a part of western Canada. In the 1870 census, taken when Manitoba became a province, out of every seven people five were Metis, one was white and one was Indian.

With the influx of white settlers after 1870 a definite snobbery emerged on the part of white people. They could not accept what they called the "dark sisters," the "heathen" families. That was a big joke because it was the Metis people here who started the churches! They were the doctors and lawyers and everything else. There had to be people to do those jobs, so they did them. It's ironic that the same

women who raised the money to build the church, who were the Sunday School teachers were, twenty years later, unpopular because of their dark skin. As a matter of fact it became unpopular to even talk about being Metis; you'll find many of the fine families of Manitoba who will say they have been here for a hundred years and won't stand up and say they are Metis. But we are Manitoba's heritage.

The history of the Metis and Manitoba is an incredible panorama with many things happening at once. In the early years of our history there were bitter arguments over who had control over trade and land. The French had one way of divvying up the land: they divided it into long narrow strips leading down to the river so that everyone could have water access. The English had a different way: they chopped up the land into squares.

Trading in Manitoba was dominated for a long time by the Hudson's Bay Company. Then the Northwest Company, which was mainly further west and in the States, moved into Manitoba. They would deal with anybody; they were open traders, you might say. The Hudson's Bay Company, on the other hand, dealt only with Indians and with the Metis people. They wanted an embargo on other trading. This made it very difficult for people to make any money because everyone was at the mercy of the Hudson's Bay Company. The company would supply people with traps and goods, but then they could only sell pelts to the company. Finally, a trial decision lifted that ban and opened up free trade. Louis Riel was part of that.

Originally from Manitoba, Louis Riel was studying to be a priest in Montreal. He returned to Manitoba because a call went out for somebody to lead the Metis people through all the trade and land problems they were involved in. The Metis needed somebody who could talk with government officials and Riel was an eloquent, well-read, intellectual man. There was some talk at that time of Manitoba becoming part of the United States but Riel felt that the people were primarily Canadian and that the Canadian government would be a better choice.

When Louis Riel took over the government in 1869, he did it through force, but without shedding any blood. The Canadian government dispatched troops from Ottawa and Riel intended to hand over the government and bring it in as a province. Instead, Colonel Wolsley lost control of his troops and one prisoner, Thomas Scott, a man with a violent past, was shot and killed by Riel's provisional government. The white population went crazy because Scott was a white man. They felt that this was the start of a bloodbath, that people were going to be shot, when in fact it had been an unfortunate mistake. There were riots in the streets and Louis Riel fled for his life and lived in the United States for a number of years.

Louis Riel

In 1885 Riel returned, this time to Saskatchewan. Again, people were suffering because there was no government, no protection. Even the white population was starving. When Riel went out among the people he spoke of nonviolence and said there would be no guns. But Gabriel Dumont and the others who had encouraged him to come to Saskatchewan were very good at guns. The government brought in Gatling guns and started attacking and there was a bloodbath at Batouche. Finally they caught Riel, hanged him and shipped his body back to Manitoba, where he is buried in St. Boniface Cathedral. Every year in November there is a service there and the Metis people remember his death because despite the violence of the time, Louis Riel embodied their hopes and dreams: the dream of a free land, of an economic base on the land, of order, of food for everyone—the dream of a land where people without power would not be subjected to the tricks

of companies. 1985 marks the centennial of Riel's death and the Metis people are planning a special arts and cultural exposition to observe it.

In Manitoba, land claims called scripts were given away to Finns, Icelanders, Ukranians. No restrictions were placed on any nationality other than on the Metis and many Metis people found it very hard to actually take over their own land. So they would just put the script in their suitcase and move, or just throw it out. As a matter of fact, parts of Winnipeg were part of the Metis' original script and the titles have never cleared. If it had been any other nationality this situation would have caused all sorts of court cases. Right now, however, the Manitoba Metis Federation is seeking justice over one hundred thousand acres that were scripted to Native people which never went to Native people.

One thing that really irks me is when people say that the reason Native people haven't progressed is that they fight among themselves. I would like to see the government say to all the English: Stand up and tell us what your political views are, and unless they all match, we are not going to do a thing for you. Of course it's impossible. You cannot make everybody believe in the same thing. But people expect us to do things that are impossible for the rest of the population to do.

We take pride in ourselves; we take pride in the fact that we are a blend. We feel that we belong to the land and that we are part of the people of Canada. Wood smoke and sweetgrass are two rural fragrances. Wood smoke stands for *Boise-brule* and sweetgrass is burned in the Indian ceremonies, and both of them rise up in the air. Sweetgrass is used as a prayer. The smoke in the air is a prayer. We Metis look back to our past and say: This is what we are. This is a reminder of our past and our traditions and culture. At the same time, it means looking forward, offering a prayer for the future, hoping that our children will have an even better life and go on to better things.

"I'M A GUEST IN MY OWN HOME!"

Mary Two-Axe Early

I was brought up by my grandparents here at Caugnawauga. My grandfather was a dominion constable, a policeman, for thirty years on the reserve. When he died, and when my grandmother died later on, friends of mine said, "Let's go to New York for the winter." That's how Indians were at the time. The men were steelworkers and they used to go to New York and do steel work, so we went too, because we knew a lot of Indian families there.

Three of us young girls all married American fellows. Before I got married I went back to the reserve and went to our band council and I said, "I know all about the Indian Act." My grandfather had been involved with the government and legal things and I knew that by marrying a white man I would lose my status. I told them, "I'm going to marry this American and I'm going to leave the reserve."

Well, the chief at the time (this was in 1938) said, "Oh, you're going to marry a stranger. How do you know how he's going to treat you? What if he deserts you in the middle of the city? Where will you go? No, you keep your little home and little farm. You never know when you'll come back to it. Who knows?"

So I got married. Two years later I had a little boy and then four years later, a daughter. I spent my summers on the reserve. Every summer. Nobody said anything. Everything was okay. I was married to a white man but everybody knew me.

Mary Two-Axe Early lives on the Caugnawauga Reserve near Montreal.

And then it started all of a sudden, when Jeanette Laval fought to get back her status as an Indian, which she had lost by marrying a white man. She took her case to the Ontario courts and she lost, so her lawyer pushed it to the Supreme Court of Ontario and she won. They said that she ought to get her rights back. But the Minister of Indian Affairs brought it before the Supreme Court of Canada. That was a big thing—it spread across Canada, about this Indian woman fighting for her rights in the Supreme Court. In the end, she lost. Five judges were against her and four in favor.

After that, all the men seemed to come alive on all the reserves across Canada, saying, "The women who are married to outsiders don't belong here. They can't inherit, they can't send their children to the government schools on reserves, they can't vote, they can't do anything—they're outsiders." That's how it started. Then they started telling us women, "You have to give up your property. Give it up to somebody, a relative, or sell it outright."

So we decided to complain to the government and take it before the public, saying, "We don't like this law! This law wasn't made by Indians; it was made by the government."

It was just luck that the Royal Commission on the Status of Women was meeting that year. Through ads in the newspapers they invited any women's groups to send them a brief. So we wrote a brief and sent it to Ottawa and they liked it so much they sent for us. They couldn't believe what was happening to Native women who had married outsiders. After they heard us in Ottawa, they said, "Your brief is important; you'll be heard the last week."

So we went to Ottawa. We had to hide to leave the reserve. Our bus was put in the churchyard and my son-in-law took the women to the bus, one at a time—there were thirty of us. It really was *terrible,* you know, to go against the band and the government! Anyway, we went to Ottawa, and the women told how they feared they would be evicted. Their children couldn't swim in the local swimming pool because they weren't Indians anymore, even though the children of Indian men who were married to white women could. The people on the panel in Ottawa were shocked.

We came home in the middle of the night—we were afraid to come home. And the next day, oh my goodness, the men were mad! How dare we, how *dare* we complain about the Indian Act? They didn't realize that we come from a matriarchal society where the women were important, the bearers of clans; women taught the culture, the language. They didn't even think of that—they were on the British side, where the male is the only leader.

That all happened in 1973. In 1975 we started writing briefs to different government officials. They wrote back saying that they supported us but it was the law and it was very hard to change a law.

In 1975 I was invited by the Canadian women delegates to attend the International Women's Year Conference in Mexico City. I planned to say something about the situation of Native women in Canada. By that time I was getting mail from across Canada. One senator in British Columbia wrote, "Mary, you should see what's going on in Vancouver, on skid row, where the majority of prostitutes are Native women. They're in and out of prison and it's costing the province more money than if we gave these Native women back their rights so they'd be able to go home. A lot of their parents want them to go back but the band council says, 'No, the Indian Act says you lose your rights if you marry a white man, and a child by a white man isn't welcome.' " All this I was going to tell.

But I didn't get a chance. None of the Canadian delegates were able to get to the podium. The Canadians met every morning and a few days before it was over, the women said, "We're not getting anywhere with what we want to say. Let's concentrate on *Mary's* problem; let's see if we can do something about that." But the National Indian Brotherhood, as they were called then, had sent two women to see if any Native women were going to complain or talk about their problems. They must have told people in Ottawa who phoned my chief on the reserve, because that night when I phoned home my daughter said, "Mother, we have a houseful of people sitting here. We weren't going to tell you because you might have a heart attack, but a friend of yours in Ottawa suggested that we tell you: you've been evicted. The police came and brought your eviction notice and you have sixty days to get out of this town." Just leave. . . have to get out. . . I'm trespassing. . . Then, of course, I got excited.

The next day when the Canadian delegates met I told them what had happened. "I've been evicted from my home," I said, "because I'm *here*. And I haven't even said anything yet!" The women got mad, "Now we're going to *really* say something."

In the meantime, some third world young people had been sneaking up to the podium; they had their problems to tell, too. And when the Mexican president's wife spoke she got booed. A young man grabbed the microphone and we jumped up and said, "Can we talk? We're Indians from Canada." He said, "You're Indians? Okay." The only reason he let us

talk was because we were Indians.

So I got up and I told them what had happened to me. An Indian girl who was studying law read the section of the Indian Act where it deals with women and then a French women from Montreal read telegrams that had been sent to the Prime Minister and the Minister of Indian Affairs and asked if the whole assembly would approve. Of course they all stood up and shouted and approved. Then the newspapers took it up and when I got back there was publicity and all kinds of TV coverage telling what had happened.

The Minister of Indian Affairs was annoyed with the press; he told the chief to withdraw my eviction because it was causing too much publicity. So the chief said I could stay here, but be sort of quiet. Naturally, I didn't agree to that. So we went ahead and went to court and right now I'm still in Federal Court over the eviction notice. It's been in Federal Court since 1975 or 1976, and here it is 1985. They keep putting my notice under; I guess they're embarrassed. The lady who is being evicted with me is eighty-one now, and I'm seventy-two so it's going to look pretty ridiculous, eh? You know, being evicted from your home, and for what? Because you went to Mexico City?

Well, this is how far *my* story goes. After that, I kept on meeting Canadian women. They've been wonderful because they're the ones who really helped us with the politicians. I've been to colleges and the students have been great. I tell them, "All I ask you to do is write letters."

The men don't want to change the Indian Act because they have the best deal. If a couple owns property and they die, everything goes to the son and nothing to the daughter if she's married to an outsider. The men like that: they get the property. Back in the 1800's, when the government wanted to assimilate the Indians, they knew they would have to get rid of the women, the childbearers, the culture teachers. They figured that if you take the Indianness away from Indian women, well, the men would start marrying white women and the first thing you know, there'd be no more Indian culture.

I think all the energy we've put into this struggle has been good. I get mail from women who thank me for speaking up, because really, from 1973 until now, women have been afraid to speak up. If you're on a reserve they can tell you to leave and no one can help because it's illegal. The Indian Act says it: you're trespassing. That's why a *lot* of women left before *we* started to do anything. They would get a letter saying they had to leave and they would sell their property quietly because they were so ashamed. I lost a lot of friends here when I started because they were afraid to be associated with me. When women supported us, their husbands told them to mind their business. But now I'm starting to get my friends back because it's out in the open.

Now they have started to bring back the old traditions: Women should be heard, should be respected and all that. It's very good but I don't like this Long House, their religion. My brother's family turned Long House and they had white teachers, too, who taught what wrongs religious people had done to Indians— how they'd taken their land. They taught them that no religion is any good except the Long House. They honor the Great Spirit and *that's* God. They sit around and smoke a pipe. . . I mean, there's not that much *to* it.

My grandparents followed a lot of the old Indian traditions. My father and my grandfather were medicine men, herbal men. The women were still important then, before it changed. My older grandson,

fifteen, likes being Indian. The other one doesn't like to be Indian. I try to teach them to speak the language but what can I teach them about the culture now? We eat Indian food only once or twice a week. They can't make bark canoes or anything here; there's nothing growing.

I'm hoping I can be buried on the reserve. If I die and I'm not buried here I know the Montreal press is really going to push it. They're waiting for me to die, I guess, to see what's going to happen to my body! Well, after sixty-five you're living on borrowed time, I believe.

All that we want is the right to stay here and not be harassed or threatened, just live in peace and be able to be buried on the reserve. That's it! We're all living in homes that were left to us by our families. With me, my daughter married an Indian from Caugnawaga so she was lucky. I left her this home and I'm living with them now, and her three boys. But my son-in-law could get mad at me and tell me to leave and I'd have to. So I'm a guest in my own home.

By allen

"WHEN ASSIMILATION IS ATTEMPTED, WE SAY NO."

Tom Sampson

I was raised by my great-grandmother. There were twenty-two people living in her house. We slept on the floor, got water from a spring well. I didn't go to school until I was seven years old. My first language was Coast Salish. I was about eight when I started to learn English.

My dad worked in the logging companies following the harvest in the United States. Even after my parents got their own home I stayed with my great-grandmother most of the time. After grade eight I went to St. Louis College in Victoria for a couple of years, then I quit and started to work for a logging company. Eventually I went back to school and took up public administration.

There are about four hundred and fifty people living on our reserve. At the time the government allotted land to our tribe we were totally dependent on the ocean as our source of food. They gave the coast Indians small parcels of land because they figured that since our livelihood came from the ocean we didn't need much land. Something like twenty acres were allotted per family, no matter what size family. As a result, our villages are very small.

I guess my prime motivation for getting involved in politics was getting married and having children. I became concerned about the community and I wanted my children to have a better education than I had, more opportunity and a better life.

Electricity came to the reserve in the late forties or early fifties but a lot of our people did not want it. They had become afraid of the government because every time we took something from the government they said they were paying us for the land, so a lot of our people did not want to get involved. They did not even want family allowances or pension checks. Some of our people never cashed pension checks because they were afraid that it was payment for the land; the checks would come in and they just kept putting them away. In those days there was no clear understanding about money. We were independent. We hunted. We fished. We really did not need much money. I am talking about the twenties, the thirties, and even into the early forties.

People also became suspicious of the government because of the way we were treated. For example,

Tom Sampson is Chief of the Tsartlip Indian Band, Brentwood Bay, Vancouver Island, British Columbia.

policemen would come to the reserve and kick open the door of your house to see if anyone was drinking. In our little house they would just walk in, make us all get out of bed when we were sleeping, take out blankets and scatter them on the floor, turn our mattress upside down and in some cases they even opened the mattress. Our people were not even allowed to leave the reservation without permission from the Indian agent. Many of our people ended up in jail for years for carrying on the tradition of potlatch. So all these things were on our minds when all of a sudden the government decided they wanted to start giving us money. It was sort of weird: Why, after all this torture, did they start giving us money? So people were very reluctant and suspicious.

I remember, when I was a boy, how the Indian agent would deliver a box of groceries once a month: a bag of flour, some brown or white beans, some baking soda and lard. It was called rations. I guess he got tired of doing that because eventually they gave us pieces of paper called vouchers. We would go to the store and the storekeeper would point to the box of groceries with our name on it, we would pick it up and walk out the door. Then finally the guy must have gotten tired of packing our groceries for us so they decided to give us checks—relief checks, they were called in those days. They were for twenty dollars for a month, I think, and we were allowed to buy groceries. When we reached a certain amount the clerk would say, "You just better take some candies or chocolate bars to fill up the amount for the check." As I got older I began to understand that it was terribly, terribly humiliating to have to accept food that you didn't want and not be able to decide how to spend the last nickel.

I got into politics when I was twenty-three, some twenty-five years ago. I have been chief for eight elections and have represented the chairman of our tribal council for British Columbia for two years. As regional chief I hold the portfolio for constitutional issues for the status Indians of Canada.

When I first was elected chief, there were only three houses on the reserve that had indoor plumbing and water. Now we have finished installing the proper facilities in all the homes in the village. Then we got involved with the government for medical services. Our children were having problems with their teeth and eyes and we were able to cooperate with some of the schools and health units within the provincial system. Since then we have run into difficulty because the federal government has been slowly withdrawing its financial support of the provinces. And it's clear that the province is not going to do anything on our behalf unless they receive money for it.

We have started to discuss the issue of education with the federal government. Our children were being put into vocational or occupational skills programs when some of them were qualified for academic education. My wife and I started organizing committees in our own village and other villages and we eventually unified and complained. Then we did get some help from the federal government.

Another thing we have been able to do is establish a better quality of housing. When the government was building the houses on the reserve they had one standard model and no matter where you went in Canada they had the same floor plans. We told the government that we wanted to build our own houses and we started to hire our own men. We established training programs and now we have our own plumbers and electricians to do most of the wiring and plumbing on the reserve. The government has finally started to understand that we are quite capable of holding a hammer and managing money.

Another change is that the people who are involved in the administration of the reserve are getting training in financial accounting; some of them are even into computer financing.

These are some of the changes that we've made over the years and I think the public is starting to realize that many of our young Indian people have great potential and are capable of making a contribution—not only to our own community but to the non-Indian community as well.

Three years ago the Assembly of First Nations (AFN) was organized; our tribal council was one of the strongest leaders in getting it established. The Joint Council of Chiefs, along with the National Indian Brotherhood, organized the AFN. Once the new assembly was in place, each region elected a regional chief or vice-chief. I was elected by the chiefs of this province to represent them on all matters concerning the affairs of our people. As I mentioned, I was put in charge of the political portfolio, which includes constitutional issues regarding the Indians of Canada.

Even though to this day many of our people don't want any part of the constitution, most of the chiefs are involved in discussions with the federal and provincial governments. We have done research to describe the process by which Canada first acquired North American land and the process Canada had to follow once it became a confederation. The Royal Proclamation of 1763 laid some of the groundwork, but this was only one treaty. We have looked at old treaties and new treaties for a clear understanding of what treaties mean.

The educating of the non-Indian is probably the hardest thing we have to do. For too long, the government and the people of Canada did not think we were capable of representing ourselves, whether at a constitutional table or any other forum. The Royal Proclamation of 1763, for example, was not designed for the benefit of Indian people, but for people coming to this country; the process that it sets out makes it very clear that before land could be acquired, there had to be consultation and consensus. The Royal Proclamation came at a time when Canada was involved in a seven-year war and was totally dependent on the Indians as allies. After they won the war certain agreements were supposed to be honored but unfortunately, the English did not live up to their part. As a result, Indians went to war with non-Indians. Since they were in the majority, the Indians could have won the war. The English knew this, so the proclamation was established. Our willingness to sit down with the government as far back as 200 years ago was a clear signal that it was important to negotiate with Indians on any settlement.

I am optimistic as heck about the future. The people who are in power now are going to go away and the younger generation is going to be a lot more realistic. Children who are growing up now have a better understanding of the non-Indian and they will probably change the minds of the next generation. So time is on our side. We're going to be here for the next thousand years or more. My forefathers felt the same way. We were raised the way we were so that we would survive these onslaughts. And when assimilation is attempted, intending to wipe out our entire race, we say *no*. We have no problems with integration. We don't mind sitting down in the same room, going to school, working with you, but don't try to assimilate us. Our people are very religious and it is that type of faith and hope that has allowed us to survive up to this day.

The only thing I can say, in summing up the whole issue of the Indian people of Canada, is that this is our land. It belonged to us in the beginning and no one can prove any different because they would have to go back to the Ice Age. The formula by which our people have managed to survive is based on things that we haven't said yet, things we will never be able to tell you. In the end, I am positive that we will get justice. It may not be in my time, but it will be in my grandchildren's time.

ON THE LINE

Sign, sign, on the dotted line
and you will be mine forever
and ever, like the mountains
and the lakes, the sky
the soil and everything I take.

I will supply you with all
of your needs: a medicine chest
a school, a bible, a blanket
rations and beads.

If you can't understand me
don't worry or whine
heed what I say
what is yours is mine.

So sign on the line what more
can be said, my word is law
you have nothing to dread.

You can't resist so don't
even try, I have cannons
and armies and cities and spies.

O, yes, I do have a home
it is far far away
but I like what I see
and I've decided to stay.

Armand Ruffo

*Armand Ruffo has lived close to his mother's Ojibway heritege
and has also lived with his father's relatives in Italy. "I am a Metis
Canadian in the contemporary sense of the term."*

Eight Northern Pueblos from San Juan Pueblo performing at Curve Lake Reserve in Ontario.

"THE BURNING CEDAR IS LIKE THE INCENSE OF THE OLD TESTAMENT"

Douglas Long

I'm a full-blooded Winnebago Indian from the state of Wisconsin. I attended grade school and high school in Wausau, Wisconsin. I graduated from high school in 1952. From 1952 to 1956 I was in the U.S. Marine Corps and got an honorable discharge. Since then I have been working in and around the Wausau area.

I've been an active member of the Native American Church since I was nine years old. Since 1962 I have been very active, attending all the international conferences, and in so doing making many friends and becoming acquainted with our history. In 1976 I became a national officer of the church. In 1982 we had our national conference up in Red Pheasant, Saskatchewan and I was elected president of the Native American Church of North America.

The purpose of this church is to foster and promote religious beliefs in Almighty God and in the customs of Native American tribes throughout North America; to promote morality, sobriety, industry, charity and right-living; to cultivate a spirit of self-respect and brotherly love and unity among the church's members throughout North America; and to maintain the right to own property for the purpose of conducting church business and services. As a people, we place explicit faith, hope and belief in

Douglas Long is president of the Native American Church of North America.

Almighty God and declare full, confident, everlasting faith in our church, through which we worship God. Furthermore, we pledge ourselves to work for the protection of the sacramental use of peyote.

The Native American Church is a national organization which has state and local chapter affiliates. Our estimated membership is around six hundred thousand people. Most members are from the Native American Church of Navajo land. There you have about three hundred thousand members; the Native American Church of North America makes up the difference, which includes the fifty thousand member Native American Church of Oklahoma. Here in Wisconsin we have approximately six hundred members in eight local chapters which are affiliated with the Native American Church of Wisconsin.

A tepee, in the past, was made of buffalo robes or bark from a tree, but we now use regular canvas. The tepee is put up with a tripod of three poles signifying the triune God—Father, Son and Holy Spirit. Those first three poles are tied together and then nine other poles are put up around the original three so that there are eleven. These, along with two poles outside which hold the draft flaps on the tepee, make a total of 13 poles representing Jesus Christ and his twelve disciples. Inside is the fireplace. This has variations among various tribes throughout the United States and Canada. Some use a crescent, a half moon; this is where the term "half moon fireplace" comes from. It's a crescent that faces the east.

Usually the conductor, the leader of the prayer service, sits on the west side of the tepee. He has a helper because we use a drum and a staff, also a gourd, a drumstick and a feather. On his left is an incense burner, called a cedar man because most tribes throughout the U.S. burn cedar for incense. Incense is burned after a prayer has been said, after a special blessing or after administration of the sacrament—maybe to a sick person, for a birthday, a funeral service, a wedding, Christmas, Thanksgiving, Easter or Palm Sunday. Palm Sunday is the day that we usually have our baptisms, but sometimes we have them on the person's birthday.

During these times, various rituals are performed throughout the night. The cedar man burns the cedar in the fireplace. Then they use an eagle feather to pass some of this cedar smoke, this incense, upon the person who is being prayed for in the belief that the burning of the cedar is just like the incense in the Old Testament and that the prayer will be taken to God above. To take care of the fireplace— since our services are conducted from dusk until dawn—

there is a fire man, and he sits on the north side of the doorway. The doorway always faces east.

At the beginning of the ceremony, the leader offers a prayer outside the tepee door. Then he leads the congregation and they line up from the east of the doorway towards the east, completely around the tepee. The leader enters from the north side of the tepee through the doorway, leading the rest of the people. Then they all take their seats.

At midnight, water is offered. It is brought into the tepee and a special prayer is offered over it. Then the fireplace is prepared. Water is sacred; it is used with prayers because it sustains all life on this planet. After the ceremony of the water, one of the elders may speak about the reason for the meeting. Then the singing and the drum continue.

From the beginning of the evening the staff and the gourd, the drumstick and the drum are passed to all male members who are seated around the fireplace. They sing praises to God—thanksgiving, honor and glory to God and his son Jesus Christ and the Holy Spirit. Prayers are offered by various people under the direction of the prayer leader.

At 3 a.m. another special stop is made, signifying Jesus Christ going into the Garden of Gethsemane and asking his disciples to stay awake and watch. At that time the cedar man prays for the whole congregation and the beneficiaries of this prayer service. Singing is then continued until just before daybreak. Water is called for again, and soon after that the prayer service is concluded. Everyone comes out of the tepee, breakfast is served and then fellowship is enjoyed by everyone until as late as they want to stay during the day.

In the beginning, the Native American Church was not fully Christian. For the past six thousand years the Aztec and Mayan Indians of South America were known to use peyote. Around 1600, with the influence of Christianity, the elders realized that many of the teachings of the Native American Church coincided with the teachings of Christianity. For instance, name giving really coincides with baptism, giving you everlasting life. It means that the Great Spirit will call your name on Judgement Day, as in the Book of Revelations. That is why elders way back in the 1600's, 1700's and 1800's began to adapt Christianity to Native American Church ways.

It is known among many church members that peyotism began in the Southwest, moved through the southern plains into the Midwest and upward through the northern plains into the Northwest. The Native American Church of the United States was organized in 1950 in order to protect the use of our sacrament peyote in a bona fide religious ceremony.

The use of our sacrament peyote corresponds to the use of bread and wine in the church. Just about all of our chapters have had problems concerning the use of our sacrament. We have had to present test cases within the states themselves to open up the use of peyote for our religious ceremonies. In 1970, the federal Food and Drug Administration, in categorizing all herbs and vegetation, came across peyote and without consulting with the Native American Church or other Indian groups, characterized peyote as a dangerous substance. We have obtained exemption within the state of Texas, which is the only place in the continental U.S. where peyote is grown. We have also been able to legalize the use of peyote in Wisconsin, Illinois, Iowa, Minnesota, North and South Dakota, Nebraska, Kansas, Oklahoma, New Mexico, Arizona, Colorado, Utah, Nevada, California, Wyoming, Montana and Idaho. When members who moved off reservations to cities started to have prayer services there, state officials came and told them peyote was allowed only on the reservation. So we had to provide a test case. We took this test case all the way to the state legislatures. In 1982, the state of Kansas opened the way for the members of the Native American Church to conduct prayer services and use our sacrament peyote in any county or township in the state of Kansas.

I am full-time clergy here in the state of Wisconsin. We have been able to have some of our leaders ordained by the Lutheran, Catholic or Episcopalian churches. I had been trained ever since I was a young boy. We do send some of our people to Cook Christian Training School in Arizona, where they get certificates of graduation and can be recognized by the councils of churches in various states. I might add that the Native American Church of Wisconsin is a member of the Wisconsin Council of Churches.

The main thing I am working on now is legislative action to introduce amendments to the Drug Abuse Prevention and Control Act of 1970. We have the backing of the National Indian Lutheran Board, we have the backing of the National Congress of American Indians and also the National Tribal Chairmans Association here in the U.S. A number of white lawyers have helped us, as well as congressmen and senators who sympathize with us in the use of our sacrament. At the present time we do not have a lot of support. But we have been able to speak for ourselves—that is why we organized the Native American Church.

"WE HAVE TO AFFIRM LIFE FOR EVERYTHING IN THIS WORLD."

ART SOLOMON

I am called a Native spiritual leader. One of the leaders of the American Indian Movement in eastern Canada came to me and asked if I would be their spiritual advisor. I said, I am a most unlikely person, but I will do what I can.

I was born and raised in Killarney, Ontario. I went to a residential school. It was something like a jail; they treated some of the children very badly. It was disastrous to take children from so far away and not allow anyone to speak their language and not allow them visits from friends or relatives. Some children went to school when they were seven and didn't see their parents until they were seventeen. We were going to become civilized Christians no matter what the cost to *us*.

Art Solomon is a Native spiritual leader who lives near Sudbury, Ontario.

About eight years ago, a friend wrote to me from one of the minimum security prisons in Ontario about the crazy world he lived in. As a result of that letter I went to visit him and took the sacred pipe to him. Since that time I have visited many other prisons and tried to respond to our people there. Because of broken homes, alcohol and drugs we live in a society that is deteriorating extremely fast. It is so tragic. Someone said, along the way, that the highest form of the political is the spiritual and I believe that is true. When I first went into those prisons with the sacred pipe I said, "They don't know what they are letting in; it is deadly for this system." And through the years, often at my own expense, I have brought into the prisons Native education with a highly spiritual content.

Many of our people in prisons are spiritually destitute. I was listening to one young women a week ago who wanted to end her life. When she looked back she felt there was nothing of value that she had done and she didn't see any purpose in the future. This individual had been robbed of all the things that give human life meaning. That's why there is such a high rate of suicide among Native people. It's not a question of money, because some of these people are from reserves that have oil and the highest income of any reserve in Canada.

A lawyer from Queen's University classified spiritual leaders who visit prisoners as missioners. Well, we are not missioners; we never will be, because that is not our way. When we go into the prisons we recognize that there are Indians with different religious backgrounds. One woman who came to me in the prison for women said she was very troubled because she found her strength in the Bible but she also respected and liked the Native traditions very much. She felt she had to go one way or the other. I said, "It's not like that—it's wherever you derive your strength. Whatever makes you a happier person, a better person, that's what you should follow." She is a much happier person today. We don't argue with people who are Roman Catholic; we don't distrust them. I've always said that whatever is good for the other person is good for us as well. But for us to cut that person adrift and say that he or she should follow the ways that are given to *us*, that would create distress and that's not right.

I am able to get into the prisons now, but it was a gradual process. Over the years I proved they could trust me, that I wasn't there to play games or bring drugs or mess around; I have proved to the authorities that I am not a dangerous person. Some of the chaplains have seen the results of what I am doing and they are satisfied and happy with it. They see in it a definite advantage for many of our people. They said what I was doing should go under "chaplaincy" rather than "social development" because it was spiritual. I have not pushed it one way or the other; I have a long-term goal, which is to bring within the prison system the right of Native people to their own spiritual ways. Practically, this means that Native spiritual leaders and medicine people would have access to the prison and that people would have access to their sacred traditions as they are practiced throughout the country. They could do a fast, have sweat lodges, sacred pipe ceremonies, sweetgrass and use tobacco. This is only a small part of the Native tradition because prisons are desecrated grounds and there are many things we won't take in.

I am now involved in what we call the Burwash Project. It is on a site that was at one time a prison; part of the property is still owned by the federal government. They were going to make it into maximum security facility for lifers, but they never did. The project is primarily for people coming out of prisons, but if I were to redesignate it, I would say it is a healing community. No one is actually living on the land but people are working the land and doing good things like thinning out trees. We propose to have that land in far better shape when we are finished with it than when we started with it.

Throughout my life I have done a great many things. I have worked in Canada to form Indian Arts and Crafts of Ontario. Arts and crafts are not merely hobbies; they are the real expressions of Indian people and a way to communicate with other peoples of the world. Fantastic and powerful communications come out of the work of Native artists. This is one aspect of the revitalization of Native people. We don't talk a great deal about Native spiritual ways, but I guess the time has come. In North America we are in the midst of a spiritual and cultural renaissance and it is very evident in the artistry of the people.

For a long time we watched strangers come to our land and live in very strange ways. Someone said that no people in the history of the human family has so devastated the world as this present society. Obviously we will either go over the cliff or we will have the good sense to turn around. And the essence of that, of course, is in Native spiritual ways. These ways were given to us by the Creator. They come from the laws of the earth, plant life, animal life, bird and fish life. The sun, the earth mother, grandmother moon, and the star world, their power has not diminished. Obviously there have been very drastic changes but it will change again, even more dras-

tically, so that order will be restored on this earth. The sun shines for every human being and we all breathe the air and we all share the same water and we are all the children of God. That is the absolute foundation of Native spirituality and it is the responsibility of every human being to choose how they will relate to the One who created all of this and who maintains our lives every day.

We don't talk about the principles of Christianity, we live them. And the first one, the most important one to me is, "Thou shalt love thy neighbor as thyself," which demands, first of all, an acceptance of each individual human being. All of us came from the spirit world and we must return to the spirit world. We have only a short journey through this part of creation so it becomes irrelevant to argue about who is "right" about religion. Our concept is that the only thing that is right (since we are spirit with a physical body) is our responsibility, individually and collectively, to respond to the One who gave us life. We are guests here of the One who created all this. And what is important is not how much you own because the only one who has the right to claim ownership of anything is the Creator.

So that is our concept and from it come the teachings of life, the creation stories of the birth of the Native nations in North America, the ceremonies, the sun dance, the celebrations, the fasts and individual purification, the sweat lodge. It is a simple way to live and if people lived that way today we obviously wouldn't have the kind of technology that we do. But I wonder if the purpose of life is to acquire that kind of technology, to lose our souls, to lose our understanding of our destiny. The first thing the average person must do is decide for themselves if they are satisfied with this world. If they aren't, then they better do something about it. Of course, in order to do anything intelligent, they have to discard the b.s. and find what is real. And they are not going to do that with radio and television.

There *is* a role for churches. Their role is to understand the dynamics of what is happening, then to make the choice of whether they want to sit comfortably blind and deaf during the little time that is left. Justice will either be done or not done. The churches can either stand with us or wash their hands of us. Ultimately, the responsibility of the individual in the community is to God. Their rights and responsibilities come from God, not from governments. We have to affirm life for everything that is living in this world.

THE MEDICINE MAN IS DEAD

He must have known the rivers still swallow,
the beak of the bird sings its morning song
and violently cries for more,
fire can either warm, burn
or consume,
there is no grimace like that which comes from
us to us

He who chanted the night
bestowing strength to the sick
visions to the unthinking
is no more—
drowned in September's water
in the flick of the moment

All the power beyond
imagination
cannot sometimes save;
no matter what the gift
the circle remains
patches of conversation continue

Quickly we shake our head
utter a word or two
discard read reread news
casually securing the door
confronting the drum of day
beating like a heart growing
into a child's face.

Armand Ruffo

A young Cheyenne

"WHAT KIND OF SOVEREIGNTY DOES AN INDIAN TRIBE HAVE?"

Thomas Oxendine

The Bureau of Indian Affairs today has a special federal trust relationship with 291 tribes, bands and groups of Indians. Under that relationship we hold a little over 52 million acres of land in trust. Treaties were entered into from the time of the ratification of the U.S. Constitution until 1871, when Congress enacted legislation that there be no more treaties with Indian tribes. But even after 1871 land was placed in trust, either under executive order or by legislative acts of Congress.

These 291 "federally recognized" tribes are tribes for which the federal government is obligated, under statutes, to carry out certain kinds of commitments. It is important to understand the things these tribes have in common with each other. To be federally recognized, a tribe has to have a governing tribal body selected by a democratic elective process. There can no longer be hereditary situations where the son or daughter of the principal chief becomes the next presiding person; it has to be a democratic process. Another thing all these tribes have in common are constitutions, tribal ordinances to determine the extent of jurisdiction that the governing body may exercise over the members. The Secretary of the Interior must approve those constitutions and ordinances.

Now, that brings up the question: What kind of sovereignty, what kind of independence does an Indian tribe have if the federal government has to approve all that? It's not necessarily how it ought to be, but the federal government requires that the BIA approve of the way a tribe acts in compliance with federal law and with the Constitution.

Each tribe is also required to have an enrollment and each determines its own eligibility criteria for membership. The federal government does not do this. It's different with each tribe: some tribes are very restrictive in their enrollment criteria, others are very lenient. For instance, some tribes will not enroll you into their structure unless you were born on the reservation. Or, you could be a full-blood Indian member of those tribes and if you marry someone outside the tribe, even though your youngsters have one-half Indian blood the tribe will not enroll them because they were born someplace else. In another

Thomas Oxendine is Public Information Officer for the Bureau of Indian Affairs, Washington, D.C.

situation we have the Pueblos in New Mexico. Male members of the Pueblos who marry outside the Pueblos may enroll their offspring without any questions, but female Pueblos who marry outside cannot have their children enrolled under any circumstances. We have one eastern band, the Cherokee, that states that if you were born prior to 1962 you must be 1/32 Cherokee blood to be enrolled. For those born since 1962, it is 1/16. A lot of people say that's not very much of an Indian. I'm not saying it is or it isn't; it's the eligibility criterion for that particular tribe. The main body of Cherokees in Oklahoma don't use "degree" of Indian blood at all; instead, you must be a bona fide lineal descendant of a member of the 1906 base roll. Their interpretation is: you *are* one of us, not *how much* you are one of us. Then we had a case go to the Supreme Court: A full-blood Santa Clara Pueblo woman had married a full-blood Navajo man. Youngsters were born to that marriage. Then some kind of accident occurred; the father was killed. The mother wanted the youngsters enrolled in Santa Clara so they would be eligible for the tribe's programs and services. But the tribe would not enroll them. Now, a tribe must be in compliance with federal law, and on the surface this does not appear to be in compliance with some of the sex discrimination laws in this country. So the whole thing got into the judicial system and worked its way to the Supreme Court. The Supreme Court ruled with the tribe, saying that the tribe does have a right to determine its own eligibility criteria for membership.

To be eligible for the programs and services of the Bureau of Indian Affairs a person must first be an enrolled member of one of these 291 tribes, and secondly, must be living on or near the trust land. If these apply, then the Bureau of Indian Affairs is responsible to ensure that those persons get the kinds of programs and services that other citizens get from their local county agencies. We are not talking about anything mysterious, we're talking about roads, law and order, schools, social services—the same kinds of things other people get.

This responsibility does not apply to state reservations where the land is held in trust by the Commonwealth of Virginia, for example, and not by the federal government. We have no relationship with Indians who live on these reservations. State reservations exist in Texas and Virginia and as established residents, Indians are subject to all the jurisdiction and eligible for all the programs there. On the other hand, once they move off the reservation, if they have a problem it's not the tribal government's problem, it's not the Bureau of Indian Affair's problem, it's the problem of the mayor or the city council or whoever handles such things at their new residence.

We know a lot more about the Europeans who came to this country than we do about the people who were already here. Through written documents we know that the Indians provided a lot of the basic subsistence those early settlers needed. They welcomed them ashore, they helped them get established; there was no problem at the beginning. But Europeans saw right from the start that there was no way they could create a society that was going to be compatible with Indian culture. European culture dictated individual ownership of land; in Indian tribes, everyone shared equally what there was. The Europeans also felt strongly that they had a more advanced civilization and that the best thing they could do would be to educate, civilize and convert the Indians to European culture. It was a utilitarian solution. Some Indians did learn the ways of the Europeans and that worked for them. Others rejected them, and this rejection led to the formation of the bureau, under the War Department, in 1824. It became part of the Department of the Interior in 1849.

I'm a Lumbee Indian. I attended all-Indian schools and never had a chance to sit in a classroom with a black or white person until I went into the Navy. I was the first Indian to go through Navy flight training. But again, one has to understand that at one time in our history we had people divided into two categories: persons free of color and persons of color. Those free of color were the country's citizens; they could own land, attend school, whatever. Persons of color were not necessarily beneficiaries of those kinds of things. Whether Indians were included or excluded depended on how regulations were written. For instance, the U.S. Army only segregated black people; Indians could attain any level in the Army if they had the skills and qualifications. At the same time, the Navy restricted the officer corps to Caucasians. So I applied for Navy flight training. I wasn't trying to change the rules, I just wasn't aware of those things.

"BEFORE THE MISSIONARIES CAME..."

Eric Anoee

Even before the missionaries and the Bible came the Inuit always believed that there was power somewhere, without knowing what kind of power. In the old days, people believed in miracles. In their lives they had seen miracles without knowing where they came from. They might have food or good health and they saw that miracle as some kind of sign, so they started believing in something.

In the old days, the Inuit didn't know anything about money when they sold fox skins or wolf skins to traders or sailors. But then they found they could get something in return; they could get material things as trade. When the missionaries came the Inuit started learning about syllabics, the way of writing. With the help of missionaries they started to understand what the Bible was all about and what the church was all about.

To my understanding there were four kinds of *anashuk* (shamans)* in the old days. One healed the sick, because in those days we didn't have any doctors. Another prayed to the Power for food and for health. A third *anashuk* protected you and your family against the enemy. And if you were against somebody, the fourth *anashuk* was a way of killing them or giving them bad luck; that was the worst kind. The

A person with special powers who acts as a religious leader or a healer.

Eric Anoee lives in Eskimo Point, Northwest Territories. He is a deacon of the Anglican Church of Canada. The translator for this interview was Mary Thompson, an Inuk on the staff of the Inuit Cultural Institute, Eskimo Point.

fourth *anashuk* was different from the rest. In some churches they believe in praying to Mary or other holy persons in the Bible. Asking something of the fourth *anashuk* was something like that, like begging for help from a special person who no longer lived, like a grandmother or grandfather. In the old days, by praying to them, begging them for help, they believed you would get help from the dead.

The *anashuk* who was already strong would be responsible to help the young person who wanted to become an *anashuk*. It is not for just anyone, only for some people. Becoming an *anashuk* was like passing tests in school. A person would have to pass certain things; one of them was fasting. That's why only some people can become *anashuks*. When the missionaries came, the *anashuks* started to wonder if their religion was the right thing, if *anashusks* would last. They worried about their future just as we do, and they turned to the church because more and more people believed in it. It was like surrendering.

In the old days the Inuit had one leader. This person knew about hunting, what the weather was going to be like or if there would be enough animals and food. People would learn all they could from this person. It wasn't like today, where we look for entertainment and when things don't go our way we get all frustrated and upset. These were people who were happy in the way things turned out.

In the old days, everybody was kept busy; each one had something to do. Young girls would help their mothers dry skins, scrape them and get them ready for clothing, or clean the home, or make a hole in the lake to get water. Young boys would help their father get everything ready for hunting, or if there was nothing to do they would go to another home to help out. There were people who would need help, like elders or sick people, and then everybody would help them.

People lived in igloos in the winter and tents in the summer. In those days the family was important. People lived close to one another. If there was a big family in one igloo they would make another igloo with tunnels connecting them. There might be two or three connected igloos, depending on how many children you had. Parents might live in the main igloo and a son or daughter and their family were in a connecting igloo. Older people, like grandparents, lived in a separate igloo. The father made the igloo. If the snow was not that good, the bottom part would be the snow and they would cover it with a tent.

Once they built an igloo they would go hunting somewhere and come back to it, depending on where the animals were. One year there might be animals in one area and they would not have to move very far. Other times, when the animals would move somewhere, they would leave for a few weeks and follow the animals. In the spring, around May when the ice starts breaking, they would come down to the coast and stay there for the summer. In July when the skins are good for clothing, they would go inland again for the rest of the winter. Before the Hudson's Bay Company came, sometime before 1900, as I was told by my mother, they used to go to Saskatchewan and Manitoba maybe once a year to buy the things they needed.

People started living in this area when the government came. In that year there was starvation around Eskimo Point and the government didn't want to travel from one place to another, it took so much time. So they asked the families to move here. The other reason was that the government schools were here and the parents didn't want to have to stay away from their children when they started school. It was between 1950 and 1960 when education started in the North. The parents were told that there were other ways to make a living and that if their children went to school and got an education, they would get jobs. It's like anywhere: the parents would tell their children to go so they could make a living, a different kind of living.

The way people look at education today is good and bad. I mean, there are people who go to school and work at jobs and there are other people who would rather be hunters. If everybody goes to school they are not going to get jobs. Those who would rather be hunters should be hunters. It wouldn't be right if everybody had jobs and we ran out of meat or if everyone was a hunter and we ran out of money, so that is just the way things turn out.

Before the missionaries came, there was a trading post in Goose River. I worked there as a helper, but it wasn't five days a week in the office; I was free to go hunting, to learn what I wanted—like how the white man survives. When the missionaries came, I started learning from them how the white man lives and what the outside people believe. A few years ago I received an Order of Canada award. I was probably recommended as a good worker, a person who is interested in all things, big things and small things, and someone you can depend on.

By AF Allen

"ALL MY LIFE I JUST KNEW I HAD TO GO BACK."

Anita Dupris

I was born in Mespelen thirty-five years ago. I grew up in a small town near the reserve but spent a lot of time on the reserve with grandmother, especially during summer and winter vacations. At Western Washington University I studied French and English. I did master's work in guidance and counseling at Eastern Washington University. When I decided I didn't want to work in counselling, I took a job at the Spokane Legal Services as a paralegal worker. After a couple of years I decided I needed more training in law, so I attended law school in Spokane, completing my Juris Doctoral Degree in 1981. I worked for private attorneys until 1982, when the chief judge for our tribe called and said she would be leaving the position. This position has to go to a tribe member

Anita Dupris is the chief judge for the Colville Confederated Tribes, Mespelen, Washington. She is licensed as an attorney in the state of Washington.

and she asked me to apply to be a temporary judge. I did, and I got the job.

Our tribe has approximately 6700 members, about half living on the reserve, which covers around 1.3 million acres in the middle of Washington state. There are two associate judges and myself. We comprise the judicial branch of our government. In our tribe we practice the separation of power; not a lot of other tribes do. The judicial branch interprets the statutes and codes and the legislative body, the tribal council, makes the laws. If I make a ruling they don't agree with they cannot overrule it; they have to go back and change the law. Associate judges hear cases only if the chief judge is not available or if it involves a relative of the chief judge.

We have a whole criminal code and we exercise criminal jurisdiction over all Indians who live on the reservation or who come to the reservation and commit offences. We handle civil cases involving resident against resident, contract action, civil guardianships and other types of general civil actions. The first laws that we apply are tribal laws. We have a whole law and order code as well as case law that has evolved over the last few years. We have also applied custom law in certain situations. If we have nothing that speaks to a specific situation, we can look first at state law and then at federal law.

Because I am not an elder, I cannot go around saying I know exactly what our customs are. When we have to make a decision based on custom law it usually has to be written down—that's the sad part. But in order to help, we have a section in our code that says I can call a panel of elders as advisors. In one instance, I had each of the parties call two of their elders, and I called two, and all these elders come into court. I did not come in as a judge because I cannot hold myself higher than they. When I went back to the notes and tapes I tried to figure out if that is our custom and how it applied to the legal issue before me. It took a long time.

Custom law does sometimes conflict with other laws. In fact, one decision I made was in direct conflict with tribal, state and federal law. The question was whether grandparents have the right to be notified in adoption proceedings. What had happened in this case was that both parents had died, but before they died the father, the second to die, gave the child in question to his sister. After his death she initiated adoption proceedings and the maternal grandparents were not given notice of it. They had no right to notice under any law, state or federal, but they appealed the adoption. The elders indicated that under customary law they should have been involved. So we had a hearing on whether or not we had to vacate the adoption.

The limit on the maximum penalty that any tribal court can give is a $500 fine and/or 180 days in jail. In our code, Class A offences pull maximum penalties. These include driving under the influence, or while the license is suspended, battery, rape and gross misdemeanors. Class B is $250 and/or 90 days and includes disorderly conduct, intoxication, having an invalid motor vehicle license. There is also an appeal procedure.

Having our own legal system has helped us become better able to give the image of self-government to the dominant culture. I think our legal system is getting as sophisticated as that of the dominant culture, and in some ways, as in our customs, it is a lot better. If the adoption case had gone to state court there would have been no question at all—the grandparents would not have been able to get their custom recognized.

I see the trend of Indian law in the U.S. as more and more stringent. The Supreme Court tends to give whatever interpretation it wants. We have a Supreme Court that is appointed by the President and reflects his points of view; and since the justices are there for life, I don't see changes for a long time.

I try to keep abreast of what is going on. I can honestly say I have no real personal interest in environmental issues that affect *other* places; my position is that I can't really do anything about those things. I can be excited that other people are involved, but I'm just going to try to have an impact where I am—for example, by thinking of ways people who are habitual alcoholics can get help and get jobs. Maybe then my small impact will carry on.

It was always my goal to come back to the reservation. I think a lot of it was because of my grandmother's influence in my life. It was always, "Well, when you come home. . ." All through my life I just knew that I had to go back. When I started law school an attorney there asked me what my goal was. I was married already and I had a pre-school child, but I told him that in ten or fifteen years I wanted to go back to the reservation and be chief judge of our court. It came within two years of when I graduated—that's how much they needed the experience.

I am deeply involved in the community. Since I have a child I'm involved in the school and I sit on the Parent Indian Education Committee. I take my grandmother to all the dinners and things, so people still know me as Isabel's granddaughter. And I make pies—that's always a big seller. Last month I made almost one hundred pies for different occasions! People see me as something other than a judge because I haven't given up things I was always involved in. I hope this has a positive effect in the community. I think it makes a difference to some people that I'm a woman, too. Most of our tribal council, fourteen members, are men. One is a woman and she's been there for years. Although a lot of women are employed there are not many in highly visible top-level jobs.

That my grandmother was a strong influence on me is not surprising: I come from a family with ten children and Mom loved us all but she didn't have a lot of time to be with us. Dad worked in construction and was always on the road. There are a lot of adult people in my family to support the children. I have twenty-seven nieces and nephews. When I go to their house, because I'm one of the older ones I can play a role in disciplining and my sisters aren't insulted. We have that concept woven into our family. My grandmother has always been a strong force—she gave us all our Indian names, showed us how to prepare for feasts, prepare for funerals, how to clean the house and if you didn't do it the way she wanted it, you could start all over. She has been instructing us all this time. I was very fortunate compared to the rest because I spent a lot more time with her. She's ninety-six now and I'll never know everything I want to know from her.

"YOU'RE NOT INDIAN, THERE ARE NO INDIANS LEFT!"

Yvonne Beamer

I am Cherokee, a member of the Southeastern Confederacy of Cherokees. My people are from Virginia, North Carolina and Georgia and are non-reservated. We have very close contact, but we don't have a reservation. In fact, right now our group is going for federal recognition.

I grew up in the north central part of Pennsylvania. It was a predominantly white, working-class, farming community; very small, less than three thousand people. I spent lots of summers with Indian relatives in a more Indian community. My father is Cherokee; my mother was not born in this country and I know very little about the Arab side of my family.

I went to college in different places: Wilmington College, the University of Cincinnati and William Patterson College in New Jersey. I started as a theatre major and ended up in communications. I was always at the top of my class—never had a problem with academic standing. I worked for the Girl Scouts for four years in New Jersey and was director of the Indian Center in New Jersey for a few years. Then I moved to New York City and became assistant director for the Recruitment Training Program. When I went on maternity leave I started doing volunteer work with the Board of Education's Native American Education Program, and when they offered me a job, I took it. I've been here for almost five years as librarian and curriculum developer.

I had a background in Indian culture, not in education, so I had a lot of studying to do when I came here.

Yvonne Beamer works with the Native American Education Program of the New York City Board of Education.

We're just a little smidgen in the whole New York City Board of Education. Other educators who are associates in the Board of Education don't even know there *are* Indians in New York City and they are very surprised when we show up. Even people in high administrative levels haven't heard of our program. We'll have one little Indian child in a classroom of non-Indian children so we find ourselves involved with the education of non-Indians without wanting to be.

When I was a child I knew we were different, but it didn't really dawn on me *how* different until I was much older. I can remember how we'd be studying a unit on Indians and everything would be discussed in the past tense—"was" or "had been"—instead of the present. I knew there were Indians around and I knew that I was a part of it; something was wrong, but I couldn't put my hand up.

And then we'd see westerns at the local movie theatre and cowboys would be killing Indians. I didn't really empathize too much with the Indians—I just didn't want the horses to get killed. Maybe it was a way of escaping racism because as a kid I didn't know how to deal with it.

I can remember being called on in class to talk on Indians and how shy I was. The only Indians I knew were in my family. I was just a little girl in a small community and it was very hard for me. Then when I got older and more radical, those experiences helped me understand the nature of oppression in this country.

When I was involved in the struggle against the war in Vietnam I remember coming together with people who had the same motives and yet there was a real difference. Comments would be made by people who were supposed to be well-informed: "Listen, let's keep it down and not act like a bunch of wild Indians." If I raised an issue concerning Indians—Alcatraz, for instance—well, it wasn't as important as Vietnam. And yet the civil rights movement in the South was. It was difficult for me to accept the fact that even at that time Indians didn't mean anything to most enlightened people. I felt like I was always talking about Indian issues, but on the other hand *someone* had to raise them! I also found people in the movement who went from being racist by denying that there *were* Indians, to being very patronizing; anything an Indian would say was gospel. Yet they didn't care enough to struggle with us around the issues.

Finally I started to study and come to grips with my own history. That was difficult. First of all, it was hard to get good information. Second, there was no one to discuss it with in my school. That's why I feel that educating our Indian kids in New York City is one of the best things we can do for them, saying: Look, it's the rest of the world that's nuts—you're okay. You have all these wonderful things to be proud of!

I didn't grow up with that attitude, although I did get some of it from my grandfather. He didn't sit down every day and say: Okay, we're going to have a Cherokee lesson. He taught through his actions, when he identified different herbs and animals, when he showed respect for living things. I realize now that his Indian-ness was his gift to us.

A lot of kids in the Indian program don't have grandparents or they live far away from them; some grow up in New York City and never see trees. I used to feel that I wasn't really qualified to work with my own people. But then I realized that many Indian people grew up the way I did and that even people on the reservation may know very little about traditions. Some do; some are lucky enough to live in traditional communities. But most Indians are raised as Catholics or Baptists or Methodists, so what difference does it make? Indian religion is not separate from the culture and you lose a lot of your traditions by being raised in a foreign way, so to speak. Most of my family are Christian, mostly Baptist, but I wasn't raised in any religion since my adoptive father is a medicine priest.

When the forced removal of the Cherokees to Oklahoma began, many of the Cherokees hid out because they were afraid. It was at this time that my great-grandmother gave birth to my grandmother in a cave in Tennessee. When the Cherokees got the sign that the coast was clear and they could go back to the homelands that had been set aside for them in North Carolina, the people in my family were afraid to go back because they didn't trust the government anymore. Some people did go back, but my people eventually settled in Virginia.

The Cherokees had a treaty with the Commonwealth of Virginia but it was never actually in our possession. I went to the New York Historical Society and did some research and found a copy of our treaty there. They had signed this document and it had gotten lost. Very few people know or are willing to admit that there are so many Cherokees in Virginia. The treaty is not recognized because a lot of the Cherokees were in a position to buy land; some even had black slaves.

The Native American Education Program is part of the Office of Bilingual Education of the New York City Board of Education. Our task is to identify the Indian students in the public school system and serve them. There are a thousand schools in New York City and the Indian kids aren't all in one school; you may have three in one and one in another. We have over five hundred in the program whom we have identified ourselves. With a staff of three it's almost impossible to serve the existing kids, plus get out there and find new ones.

We offer a variety of services to the kids. We run an after-school program at this office and we also go out into the communities where the kids live. In these classes we offer instruction in every kind of Indian craft you can think of, dancing, singing, history from our perspective, cooking, etc. We help the kids with individual research projects, offer career guidance, try to get the kids scholarships and do counselling, but not psychoanalysis. We take the students on field trips to pow-wows and ceremonies. And we have a lending library and a resource center which is open to anybody designing curriculum.

When we teach American history it doesn't begin with Columbus. And when we talk about the origin of American Indians we don't just present one theory, we present six or seven. We go into various geographic areas and explore, for instance, how and why the Ojibway started in this part of the country and then ended up migrating further west.

Sometimes it's difficult for the younger ones to get a handle on it all, so we start with food; maybe a little cooking class with a discussion on why the people in this area ate this particular kind of food and why this food has changed somewhat. We get into history like that. We also try to show what people are doing today. For instance, here in New York City, Indians are computer programmers, they work on Wall Street, they sell hot dogs in the street—there's real variety. We also deal specifically with the history of Indians in New York City. Why did Indians come to New York? What employment backgrounds do the kids' parents have? What was it like back home? Why did people have to leave? We talk about things from an Indian point of view because the kids are getting all the wrong ideas in their classes.

In the public school system they deal with other groups in literature, games, and songs. They deal with us in social studies. They feel that our point of view is just an opinion, and that their point of view is "history." Students react to this in different ways. Some don't want to be identified as Indians; some become angry, but the anger is unfocused. A lot of students take it out on themselves.

Before the inception of this program we found out that there was a 70 to 80 percent dropout rate among

Indian high school students nationwide. That rate has now decreased by 50 percent. Even in New York City we find a lot more of our kids going on to secondary school. We think they have more of a sense of who they are through this program—because before, you know, they were told in school that first of all, Indians are all dead, and the ones who managed to survive live west of the Mississippi. Then, because our kids look a variety of ways, they were told: You can't be Indian, you don't *look* Indian. What does that do to a kid's self-esteem? We had one little Indian girl who took something to school for "show and tell"—a rattle or some Indian ornament—and her teacher berated her, saying, "Why are you bringing this in? You're not Indian, there are no Indians left." We've had kids who were ridiculed in class by other students and the teacher didn't protect them.

The New York City that welcomes cultures from all over the world has some of the most narrow-minded people. If you're up in Harlem and you start screaming "nigger", forget about getting out of there alive. But if you're in Harlem where some of our Indian students go to school and you start screaming, "You stupid Indian," what's going to happen? Maybe two kids are going to get excited about it. You don't have the force here.

Indian life has also been too romanticized. The media have really hurt us in the sense that people never meet Indians except on their TV sets. I don't think Indians are picked on just because we're Indian, though. I think it's part of a larger scheme in this country against women, against blacks, against Puerto Ricans, against poor people of any color. It's *easier* to discriminate against us because there aren't as many of us, we're spread out, and when it comes to organizing, we're three hundred and some different groups.

You can't speak about Indians collectively. You can speak for Indian rights, but we're so different— and there are Indians like my own group that some other Indians don't even recognize because we're not reservated. But there are so many hundreds of little Indian groups that have survived and they're just *out* there, maybe just two or three hundred people. Their language has been destroyed, and probably their culture, but they still have maintained their Indian-ness, they are still Indian, and they get mad when they are mistaken for anything else.

In our film catalogues there are pages and pages on the Holocaust and what happened to six million Jews. (Mind you, they seldom mention all the gypsies who were annihilated by Hitler.) It was a horrible thing and I'm not saying it wasn't, don't misunderstand me. But we had millions *more* Native Americans killed and we never talk about it. There are maybe three films in the film catalogue on Native Americans. In South America, where Indians are still being killed, it *is* a holocaust. I like to compare us to the Jews, to show that we have this similarity. But the Jews kept their languages, they had people around the world who supported them, they maintained their religious symbols—and all that was taken away from us. There were over a thousand tribes at our first contact with whites and now there are only three hundred or so left. It's only been in the last twenty years that we've seen a resurgence of Indians being proud and people who are mixed-blood admitting, "Well, I *am* Indian!"

"ECONOMIC PROGRESS HAS TO BE PART OF THE OVERALL SCENARIO."

David Lester

I'm Creek Indian, originally from Oklahoma. I got my college education at Brigham Young University and graduated in 1967 in political science. After a short period of working for a financial institution in Los Angeles I went to work for the National Congress of American Indians as an economic development specialist and served that organization for about a year and a half. While I was there I worked on two major projects for the organization. One was a series of Indian trade shows to promote Indian reservations as locations for private industry, to help create jobs on the reservations. I also worked on a national study to look at the feasibility of establishing a National Indian Development Bank.

From there I went back to Los Angeles and became president of the United Indian Development Association, a non-profit organization devoted to the promotion of Indian-owned enterprise in California. During the eight years I was there, we grew from one office in Los Angeles to three offices and a state-wide program with Indians in urban and rural communities as well as on reservations. We have been able to assist in the development and expansion of over five hundred Indian-owned businesses in the state and to increase the gross sales of Indian enterprises by

David Lester is executive director of the Council of Energy Resource Tribes.

about five hundred percent. The organization is still going strong and doing an outstanding job, not only in California but throughout the U.S., with some work in Canada as well.

I was then appointed by President Carter to head up the Administration for Native Americans, which is an agency within the Department of Health and Human Services. The agency was devoted to the concept of Native Americans' economic and social self-sufficiency. We worked not only with Native Americans, but with the Native people of Alaska and Hawaii as well. A new programmatic and policy direction was developed for the agency, moving away from the concept of offering social services to the concept of economic and social development. From that developed a solid basis for legitimatising Indians' aspirations in terms of political, economic, social and cultural development along their own paths, since each tribe, each Native community, has to have its own sense of direction, its own sense of history. That's an important element in the long-term development of any community. So we were able to break away from a set federal program and fund projects developed at the local level and aimed at the causes of poverty and social disorganization.

Now I am executive director of the Council of Energy Resource Tribes. The council is a multi-tribal organization involving thirty-nine Indian tribes in the U.S. that own energy resources. These are primarily mineral resources, though there is a tremendous amount of potential in hydroelectric and geothermal resources as well as alternative sources of energy: wind, solar and biomass. But the primary resources are the coal, oil, gas and uranium of which Indian tribes own considerable quantities, particularly in the West.

As an organization our goals are quite simple but comprehensive and flexible enough to allow for many changes in the environment. These goals are to help tribes manage and develop the natural resources they own in a way that is compatable with *their* economic, cultural and political goals and within the context of their local capacity. They need the kind of technical assistance that will allow them to develop their own capabilities—that's why they formed us and that is basically what we are engaged in now.

We have a staff of geologists, engineers, environmental scientists, an accountant and people with degrees in business. An Indian tribe starts the process by determining the quantity and quality of what they own. Next, they look at the economics of what they own, what environmental issues relate to any development scenario, and finally they look at

45

the possible social and economic impact on the tribe and its members. In most cases, tribes try to get a wholistic picture before they really feel comfortable with any development strategy.

Of course many companies are not sitting around waiting for a tribe to reach that point. And tribes receive, from time to time, proposals from private industry to develop a tract of their reservation, to exploit a certain mineral or resource. Tribes may then seek our assistance in analysing these proposals, determining what the negative impact might be in environmental or socio/economic terms, as well as looking at the positive side, such as job creation. This way they can get a handle on whether it is a fair and equitable proposal for them. If they are interested in moving forward, we can work with the tribe to analyse how the proposal could be improved. Then the tribe is in a position to make a counter-proposal and enter into negotiations. We don't do all the work and then tell the tribe whether it's good or bad for them—we really just become their support staff.

When tribes are major owners of substantial resources they have much more leverage in negotiating with energy companies because of their status as units of government within the U.S. There are certain tax advantages for Indian tribes that are not applicable to other private owners of mineral resources. This makes a deal more complex, more attractive to private industry. These tax advantages also create higher returns in terms of the percentage of the take. So this is one aspect that can be advantageous to both the tribe and the company, and it increases the political status of Indian tribes.

In the past, many development agreements were actually negotiated by federal agencies on behalf of the tribes. They usually used standard leases for federally-owned land as opposed to leases for privately-owned land. This reflected the view that if these minerals were leased at a lesser rate to create lower energy costs for American industry, making industry more competitive, it was for the public good. When you apply that same yardstick to Indian-owned, privately-owned minerals, it isn't applicable. Fortunately, partly as a result of CERT but more importantly as a result of the increased assertiveness and self-confidence of tribal leadership, we're not seeing those standard lease agreements being used at all today.

We also get involved in right-of-way negotiations for pipelines, transmission lines, even highway construction. In the past, these negotiations were based on the presumed market value of Indian land. Since Indian land is restricted and can't be sold it is almost impossible to use current market value to determine what the land is worth—particularly out in the desert, or where land values tend to be depressed. We felt that the standard ought to be the value of the product being transported across the land, along with the additional cost of going around the reservation. These two factors should determine what would be a fair price for a right-of-way across Indian land. In most cases, this method has resulted in ten to twenty times higher payments than the results of the old method of trying to come up with the market value.

Indian people have always been pragmatists in addition to being spiritual. They have always had a strong will to survive. Even prehistorically, Indians mined and burned coal for domestic use. The use of nature to benefit people is not an unknown value in Indian societies. On the other hand, they have a built-in respect for nature that goes beyond asceticism to the heart of who we are as human beings. This puts a totally different perspective on the way tribes make decisions.

Our experience has been that there is very little polarization over development *versus* nondevelopproposal from an energy company. You don't see polarization over development versus nondevelopment, the way you see that occurring in non-Indian society. You do see people reaching a consensus, saying, for example: That mound is too sacred and it doesn't matter *how* valuable the resource is under the ground! On the other hand, they might say that there are other parts of the reservation that could stand some development as long as we know it will be restored to A, B or C level. This wasn't true when you had a third party negotiating on behalf of an Indian tribe, someone who may have had little respect for that tribe's internal value system. In the 1960's and early 1970's, some deals were cut which did create a lot of controversy. And in some cases development proposals can be altered to lessen the impact on sacred areas; in other cases, the tribe just says no. We have a number of tribes that are members of CERT which have essentially opted for no development at all—no oil, gas, hydro or coal mining. But they are eager to learn more about the economics and technology of the resource they own; they feel that this knowledge will give them a better understanding of the pressure to develop it.

There is a lot of tension, but one thing we are trying to do is not repeat history by letting the tension get out of hand and enter a new phase of sophisticated Indian wars, you might say. Uncontrolled conflict has already caused enough damage to both Indians and non-Indians. We want to find common ground with non-Indian institutions without surrendering the values that Indian tribes stand for. We are working, for example, on a number of round table discussions with state governors and leaders of industry to try to get them to see the issues in a new light. It is too premature to say we have found the magic key to unlock the door, but we are going to keep working at it.

This is a biased view, but I think CERT, if not the most dynamic tribal organization in the U.S., is certainly among the top three. Because of our dynamism we have some very forceful critics as well. That's a healthy sign in the Indian world. In the past, we couldn't criticize ourselves. It's a sign of maturity that we have some thoughtful Indian leadership who can criticize us without everybody feeling like we are betraying our race. Besides that, sometimes the critics are right!

I have long been interested in how Americans and Indian tribes can resolve this tradition of conflict. There must be a way America can reconcile itself to the fact there will continue to be Indian tribes as part of the overall pattern of American society. That includes not just Indian culture, but also the political reality that a tribal government does have jurisdiction over tribal land, and that when non-Indians live within the tribal jurisdiction they are under the jurisdiction of Indian government—just as when Indians move off tribal land and fall under the jurisdiction of whatever community they live in. That's something that intrigues me, and I feel that economic progress has to be part of the overall scenario as it is played out. My upbringing and my experiences as a child and a young adult have influenced that thinking considerably.

After spending a few years in Oklahoma, my family moved to California, where I went to grade school and high school. California is, you might say, a magnet—not only for non-Indian America, but for Indians too. There is quite an Indian community throughout California, including those who are native to the state and those who have moved from other parts of the country. I would have a different outlook on life if I had been raised in rural Oklahoma as opposed to southern California, which as a society is a lot more and dynamic and mobile than rural Oklahoma.

My grandmother was probably the strongest force in terms of the family's cohesion. She made sure we understood what being an Indian meant. She was active in the Indian community, on the board of directors of a number of Indian organizations, always active in social and community events. As a kid I just went along and played with other kids and got involved in cultural celebrations, sometimes called pow-wows.

The other very important thing in my upbringing was that we never had a sense that being Indian was anything less than a privilege. The stigma of being a minority group—poor, and all that—just didn't seem to stick with us. It was partly my grandmother refusing to let us grow up feeling we were weird or inferior in any way. That's important for any child, particularly when you reach adolescence and your pimples start popping up and you feel awkward and you don't fit in anywhere. Having that family support and the knowledge that you are a worthwhile individual is really important.

"IT WAS NOT SO MUCH THE LOSING OF THE INDIAN WARS AS THE LOSING OF THE PEACE."

Kirk Kickingbird

I'm a member of the Kiowa tribe located in Oklahoma, which is where I grew up and went to college and law school. I'm a lawyer. I was raised by my parents in the small town of El Reno, close to the southern Cheyenne and Arapaho reservation, but I spent most of my weekends in Anadarko where my dad grew up.

It wasn't until the end of grade school that I began to notice any differences. For example, all my white friends had a maximum of two sets of grandparents, while in the Kiowa tribe, the sisters and brothers of my grandparents also regarded themselves as my grandparents. You could be doing something wrong and it was sort of like lightning striking—you never knew where the discipline was going to come from. As a kid, it was hard to keep track of them all!

The most prominent member of my family was a chief named Kickingbird who was active in the 1860's and 70's. He was my great-great-grandfather. My great-grandfather was also active in tribal leadership. My grandfather died very young, but my dad was active in tribal politics and was always looked to for assistance. Since he tried to help folks out, this was what I was supposed to do; it developed out of a family pattern.

I am presently working in a public interest law firm, the Institute for the Development of Indian Law, which is primarily focused on research rather than on litigation. Its main goal is to assist and strengthen tribal governments. We've published a lot of our research to make sure that both Indians and non-Indians know the legal, historical basis for Indian rights. We're engaged in training programs in federal Indian law to help tribal governments and administrative staff work with and for tribal government. We're also working on economic development projects with the Fort Peck and Creek Tribes in Oklahoma and with the Narragansett Tribe in Rhode Island. And we're being invited to a number of conferences in Canada by tribes who are very interested in working on tribal constitution, tribal government and power issues.

One of the things we started out with at the Institute was a book called *Hundred Million Acres* that

Kirk Kickingbird works at the Institute for the Development of Indian Law.

I wrote with Karen Ducheneau in 1973. It was about Indian land problems and the need to set a minimum land base of a hundred million acres. The book focused on some common problems, such as a trustee putting Indian lands into a national forest. There is obviously a conflict of interest there, with the trustee benefitting at the expense of the beneficiary of the trust relationship. We looked at the way some negotiated settlements were not specifically missurveys, but rather misunderstandings which resulted in boundaries being in the wrong places. We also looked at the Alaskan Native land claims settlement, which constituted about forty million acres, and the problem of tribes getting small acreages in the West and along the Atlantic coast. Many of those tribes had fairly cordial relationships with the U.S. government, so their needs had been given very low priority—as a result, the Narragansett Tribe has just had their claim settled for 1,800 acres, a claim which had been pending since the early 1700's!

Then we got into other situations, for example, when tribes would know the general terms of their treaties but didn't know the specifics. Most of the treaty documentation books cost a minimum of one hundred dollars, so we broke them down into regional areas and made them available for nominal prices. Some of the early records, up to about 1880, are not very well organized in the Congressional Serial Set— the name of the documents reproduced by Congress—so we did a book to clarify those. Then we went into training programs and did books on sovereignty, jurisdictions, Indians and the U.S. Government, and the federal/Indian trust relationship.

The basic principle is that tribes have all their inherent sovereign powers *unless* they have given them up in treaties or, pursuant to the treaty obligation of the U.S., the U.S. has passed legislation which affects those powers of government. The making of the treaty is a recognition of the sovereignty of tribes.

Over the years, the powers of the tribes have diminished due to the encroachment of the U.S. Government. Some of this is based on scientific treaty terms. Some of it has happened according to the theory of the new federal trust relationship. And some is due to the delegation of authority by the tribes when they developed written constitutions in the 1930's.

The legal theory says a treaty can be changed without the consent of the other party *if* the legislation is to carry out the U.S. obligation of the treaty. And since laws and treaties are the supreme law of the land, a later treaty can supercede an earlier law, and a later law can supercede an earlier treaty.

Whether that can be done or not is a political issue that needs to be settled between the tribes and the federal government.

Some of the activities of the Bureau of Indian Affairs don't have a legal basis. An administrative regulation may appear that doesn't really have authority from any statute. That situation is very easy to challenge—sometimes lengthy, but easy. And there is a good deal of it. One tribe in Oklahoma discovered a few years ago that in 1867 they had signed a treaty with the federal government agreeing that their constitution would be respected. Around 1900, the Bureau of Indian Affairs moved in and tried to terminate the tribe and bring it into the federal trust relationship. They even began appointing the chiefs. And this lasted until 1972. Then tribal members came to us and asked us to file suit on the issue, which we did, and the federal court here required the federal government and the Bureau of Indian Affairs to report the treaty terms.

A lot of smaller issues also arise out of regulations that don't have a firm foundation in the law. Back during the Nixon administration in the early 1970's, the government impounded 18 million dollars intended for education. There was no legal basis for that. So we put together a team at the request of some tribal schools and sued to have that money released and spent.

One of the things you get when the tribal leadership is aggressive and informed is the ability to deal with bureaucracies that tend to do what is easiest for them. A dramatic example was when two major tribes, the Klamath and the Menominee, were terminated in the early 1860's. The Menominee had a good sense of sovereignty and decided they wanted to stay together as a nation and as a government. They decided that the federal government was going to recognize them again, but that required the passage of legislation. In 1973, the United States Congress passed legislation to once again recognize these 2500 or so people in northern Wisconsin. Once again, it became a government-to-government relationship. The Klamaths, on the other hand, were not able to maintain that cohesion and sense of sovereignty and they are essentially out of business as a tribe today.

The political relationship between a tribal government and the federal government is basically the same as a diplomatic relationship. Of course it is much easier to intimidate 2,500 or 8,000 people than it is to intimidate, say, the People's Republic of China.

It was not so much the losing of the Indian Wars as it is the losing of the peace. Tribes got the treaties;

they were no longer a problem. And not being squeaky wheels, they did not get greased. That is why Indians have to be knowledgable and aggressive today if they are going to have their rights honored.

Most of the historical conflicts revolved around land. Some, of course, were military conflicts, but most were disputes over land rights and economic issues such as hunting rights, fishing rights, rights to gather certain plants.

The unilateral interpretation of treaties by the people at the Bureau of Indian Affairs is a real problem. There it is in black and white, in writing, and that's all there is. The tribe's oral tradition about where their boundaries are might differ by thirty miles. So they begin to research historical records, journals of the treaty commissioner or military officers who were there at the time, even the minutes of the treaty proceedings themselves—and suddenly you find out that the oral tradition was correct! The references in the treaty document itself were not complete. But if the tribe litigates to gain their rights, everybody gets enraged.

If the BIA and the Secretary of State would handle these issues rather than the Department of the Interior it would put a lot of this in a better context. In the late 1700's and early 1800's you had to have a passport to go into Indian country! In fact, until 1910 or so, the Secretary of State had control of the treaties and kept the physical documents themselves. They are now with the National Archives.

The latest announcements from Reagan about reviving government-to-government relationships are encouraging. It may be in response to Indians saying, "Wait a minute. We are not an arm of the BIA. We are not an administrative agency. We are separate governments. We handle our own affairs, and we want to!" That is what a lot of the conflict is about.

In one respect, the fewer the funds available (especially now with the Reagan administration), the more tribes are forced to pare down staff, focus on keeping only the most competent personnel and look for other ways of raising revenue than counting on the transfer payments from the federal government. Tribes are eligible for revenue sharing and black grants, the same as state governments. There are also special programs available through the Department of Education and the Department of Health and Human Services.

Some tribes are aggressively looking for ways to raise money: through taxation, through running their own businesses on the reservations and through running high-stake bingo games on reservations. As notorious as these are, they can't be regulated by the states because they are only subject to tribal law. Of course, the idea that these are making money and are not regulated by the state doesn't sit well with people. It's a Catch-22 situation; on one hand, it's: "Those lazy Indians should get some work." And now that they have some work, people are appalled that they have some income.

In Alabama, Georgia and so forth, little clusters of tribes are trying to obtain federal recognition, which carries, of course, certain educational and medical services. I think there is some cordiality to this idea since if the tribes were federally recognized the states would no longer be the sole source of funds to serve them. So it would be advantage to the state as well as to the Indians.

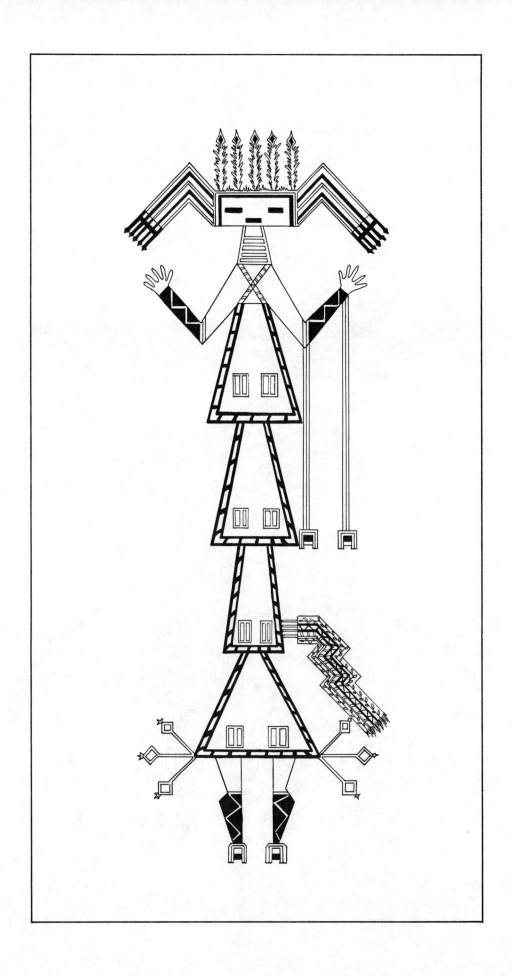

"TRIBAL GOVERNMENTS ARE THE KEEPERS OF THE CULTURE."

LaDonna Harris

I'm a member of the Comanche tribe from Oklahoma. Comanche is my first language. I was raised by my grandparents on a farm in southwest Oklahoma. My grandfather is a member of the American Indian Church and also had Eagle medicine. My grandmother was a psychic Comanche who converted to Christianity.

The fact that I was raised by my grandparents is important in two ways: First, I grew up understanding who I belong to—that I belong not only to my family, but to the tribe. I always felt that I belonged to something bigger than myself. Second, I knew that I would have to give something back to those people who made me who I am. That was never taught to me, it was just something I just grew up knowing. So I became my grandmother's daughter, the one who did things for the family and took care of the relatives. I just knew inherently that this was what I was supposed to do. Most people who are involved in Indian affairs have the same kind of feeling. It's very difficult to express, and you don't know where it came from exactly, but you know it's there and you can't walk away from it.

At Americans for Indian Opportunity we are focusing our attention on tribal government: how we come to have the governments we do, what we need to help us get through the next century and how we can incorporate traditional values into modern institutions.

LaDonna Harris is with Americans for Indian Opportunity, Washington, D.C.

We have worked with seven tribes directly and now we have the funds to take this experience out to six regional meetings. We think we will then have enough material for a textbook on tribal governments and how we fit into the political fiber of the United States.

There are a few problem areas, though. Sometimes the policies we follow create conflicts between value systems. For example, we used to do things by consensus. Now we do it by vote. Before, we didn't have winners and losers—now we do. So people may feel that by losing a campaign they have been rejected by their tribal people and they spend half their lives trying to re-establish themselves in the community. Within our own tribes we need to have long discussions and ask how we used to do things and why we have the problems we do.

The old ways are still very much known. The kind of government we have today was forced on us in the 1930's. It was well-intended because at the time, individual land allotments were killing the tribal structure. The federal government thought that constitutional government might salvage our institutions. But it also brought many social problems. First, we just ignored the new governments: we didn't need them. Then, when the Office of Economic Opportunity and all the other new federal programs were developed, people went to them and started using the constitutional government to get those funds. Our studies indicate that in the 60's and 70's, tribal governments became extensions of the federal government, administering federal programs rather than really governing the tribes themselves.

How do you evaluate all this? How do you make regulations and policies that are really instruments of the people? That fit traditional values rather than someone else's institutions? That's what Americans for Indian Opportunity is all about. And we are really at a crossroads. Everybody is talking about development and we're talking about how to govern. You just can't have development in a vacuum. We want development so people can live better, but within a community of people, the tribe. Tribal governments are the keepers of the culture—to make sure it continues to exist—because it all has to fit together. You can't separate culture from people.

Women are playing a greater leadership role in tribal offices today. They are becoming more educated and much more sophisticated. They may not be getting much national attention, but they *are* speaking out. At the same time they are plugging away in different professions, from psychiatry to the sciences.

My grandmother was a matriarch. She was the one who did the negotiating when we traded products from the farm. She was also the one everyone turned to when they had problems. She was the fabric that kept us all together. My mother had to go off to work at the Indian Health Hospital some fifty miles away. It was during the Depression and my father, who was not Indian, had too many pressures on him. He went off to California. But my mother worked at the hospital until she retired. It was my mother's generation that experienced real conflict of culture.

I have not been based at home with my family and tribe, but I have tried to do the next best thing—to do what my ability allows me to do, wherever I am. So in a way, my grandmother's role and my role are the same thing on a different scale. She drew people together, kept them working, kept reassuring everybody of their ability to deal with things. My experience in Washington is not so different: that is, nurturing, relating what I'm doing back to the tribe and the family. Keeping all that together is an important thing.

"IN THE MIDDLE OF THE TRAP LINE WAS A PAY TELEPHONE."

Jim White

I am of the Heiltsuk-speaking people who live on the coast of British Columbia midway between Vancouver and Prince Rupert. The tribe I come from is found in three distinct areas with three dialects. If you go north into the Kitamat area they are Heilslah; we in the central area are Heiltsuk; and the southern part of the tribe are Quagua-speaking people. It is probably about 450 miles from north to south—a long stretch, in terms of travelling, because it's primarily on the ocean.

My first eleven years were spent on a reserve community on Campbell Island. At the time there were a little over one thousand people; there are over thirteen hundred today. It's a mixture of Native and non-Native. I was probably of the last generation to grow up speaking our native tongue and to grow up when the traditional pattern of harvesting was still intact.

Jim White works with the Anglican Church of Canada as Consultant on Native Affairs.

In the fall, we harvested the salmon to smoke or dry; a little later in the fall it would be clam digging. Most of the elders went out to do the harvesting, leaving the middle-aged and younger people at home with the children. But during the weekend we all went out to the camps as families. Throughout the winter there was trapping and later on, in late winter and spring, halibut and spring salmon fishing and the harvesting of seaweed and herring eggs. Then in the late spring and early summer we went out fishing for the sockeye, which is the best salmon you can get.

The heritage of Indian dances and songs was still intact when I grew up. The community gathered to share and pass on the culture, the language, the customs, the songs and the myths. At that time all this was still done under a bit of stress because my people could vividly remember how the federal government, along with the churches, had attempted to do away with our language, our culture, our customs, our heritage back in the 1900's. At times throughout our history we were incarcerated if we practised our customs, and that fear remained.

The potlatch is the art of giving material goods to your guests. In most instances it follows a hierarchical system. The hereditary chiefs and the family would call a potlatch and then give material goods to the people they had invited. You would recognize people as they came in: for example, hereditary chiefs from neighboring communities would be given the most expensive gifts, like dugouts or furniture. Potlatches were given as memorials for someone who had passed away or perhaps at the birth of a child. Sometimes a potlatch was held at the time of the transformation of a child to adulthood. For a young boy, this meant going out and fasting for four days. It was expected that he would get his first game, then he would be classified as a young man so he could join the men in the community when they went out hunting, trapping and fishing. To acknowledge his achievements people were called together in the big house and there would be dances, songs and masks. When that was concluded, material goods would be brought in and shared with the people who had given their time to come and be together.

The potlatch was illegal until 1952, when it was finally removed from the criminal code. When I compare it with what goes on today, it's no different from the high-rollers on Bay Street or Wall Street—but I have never seen the federal government, the provincial government or the churches challenge *them*. They thought that our hereditary chiefs were getting very rich at the expense of the wider community, but there has never been any challenge to the well-to-do families in Canada!

I went to residential school for a year and then I went into a boarding home program and completed high school in the Fraser Valley. When I compare my village today to the way it was when I was growing up, it is like night and day. Today it is very modern—they have all the electronic gadgets that you can throw at them. Then, we only had electricity during the winter months and for no more than eight hours a day.

We were very intact as a community back then. We cooperated with one another, we celebrated, we grieved together. When we brought home food we shared it. We always looked after those who needed it—the elderly who could no longer go out and harvest, families that didn't have the boats to travel. Today, all that seems to have been taken away somewhat.

I found the English language a little difficult when I was in high school. Once I was hauled into the principal's office and questioned as to why I wasn't taking a foreign language. I told him I *was* speaking a foreign language and that I had an excellent knowledge of my native language. I was told that they didn't acknowledge my native language and that I would have to take one of the foreign languages that had been set up. Then I questioned him as to why he allowed students of German ancestry to take German as a foreign language when they were fluent in German and spoke German at home as their first language. I didn't get an adequate response.

When I was going through college in Vancouver I did a fair amount of volunteer work. I was especially concerned about my peers. I had begun to realize that on Friday and Saturday nights, week in and week out, we were all going to lounges and nightclubs. So I approached churches in Vancouver to see if we could use their hall one night a week and get a group of boys together to play basketball. I bought a trophy for eight dollars and we formed an all-Native basketball league in Vancouver. In the next few years the tournament grew to a trophy of more than 450 dollars and sixteen teams from British Columbia, Alberta and Oregon took part. And that is how I got involved with church work—it just blossomed into other volunteer activities with the church and I eventually became Consultant on Native Affairs to three churches in Vancouver. I did that for almost seven years and then in January of 1982 I was asked to be the Consultant on Native Affairs for the Anglican Church of Canada.

The churches certainly have taken a very close look at where they were in the past. Today they are very strong in aligning themselves with Native people, especially in their struggles with the government.

They have supported the endeavors of our Native leadership in the Constitutional Conference, in just land claims and other areas.

Evangelism used to mean a church would come into a community and the minister or priest would draw people into the building, saying, "This is my building. And I am administering, as a disciple, what God has asked us, through His son, to do." The shift today is that we are very concerned that Native people take leadership within our own communities and make an equal contribution to the church. And I don't think we need a big elaborate church structure to call a church service together. With Native leadership in the church we can take the content of a church service and put it into Native language, culture and heritage and offer that to the community. We are not saying that society needs to understand what we are doing. We are comfortable with it and are happy that we are making a contribution to the wider church.

Project North was started in the early 1970's by five denominations when the federal government was looking at developing the MacKenzie Valley area. They planned to extract natural resources, gas and oil, and build a pipeline going from the MacKenzie Valley Delta down south into the U.S. These plans were being made without any consultation with, or expressed concern for the Native people up there. Their lifestyle and heritage were being attacked overnight as instant towns were built. The non-Native people who arrived didn't understand the Native people up in that area. Alcohol and drug abuse increased tenfold; it had probably been there before, but to a much lesser degree.

At the time it began, Project North called for a moratorium on development and exploration until a just land claim settlement could be concluded that would satisfy everybody, both Native and non-Native. We are still fighting to ensure that the governments do follow through with their commitment; they have indicated that they are very concerned about a just settlement. *We* are very concerned about a number of areas, too. We would like to see the training of Native personnel. And we would also like to see some areas restricted for the sole purpose of retaining the traditions of hunting and trapping.

Right now we are particularly concerned about the Lubicon people in northwestern Alberta, about 65 miles northeast of Peace River. This is a small community of about 350 people. Back in 1939 they were trying to set up a land base because they had been bypassed in the early 1900's when Commissioner McKinnah went through and wrote up Treaty 8 and Treaty 11. It appears that it was too much of a challenge for the Commissioner to go into their area and sign them up in the treaty too. So they are in a Catch-22 situation today. They are Cree people, and I would say eighty percent are fluent in Cree only. The issue is that the Lubicon people are looking for land—land promised them as early as 1939. But the federal and provincial governments are playing games at their expense. The provincial government has also issued licenses for national and multinational oil companies to go into the area where the Lubicon people have traditionally hunted and trapped. We are talking about an overall living area of forty square miles and the talk is of giving them a twenty-five square mile land base to live on. But including hunting and trapping, we are talking about 8,500 square miles! They have always used this land for their hunting and trapping. Very recently, these people have started collecting welfare because the twenty-five to forty square miles in question—all they have to live on—cannot support traditional hunting and trapping. Moreover, during the last four years the companies have not only drilled for oil, they have found oil and natural gas and they are pumping even today, but the Lubicon people haven't received any royalties from this.

Project North has been able to get church groups to go up into the Lubicon area to see exactly what is happening. We got a first-hand look at the oil rigs that have been put into place and we even experienced the daily harassment that the people get from oil company personnel. A gravel road had been put in by the oil company and classified as private property. That gravel road is on an old trail used by the Lubicon people to get to their hunting and trapping areas. We were travelling on this road—there were about twelve of us in the van—with the chief of the Lubicon people driving. A one-ton pickup came towards us, right smack in the middle of the road, and he wouldn't budge over to the side. The chief was already over to *his* right-hand side and he had to veer even further over. As a matter of fact, he almost put us into the ditch. The driver of the truck did not know that national church leaders were in the van. One or two hundred yards behind us was another van that received the same treatment from the one-ton pickup. *This* van carried staff from the Canadian Broadcasting Corporation. This is the type of treatment the Lubicon people are subjected to on their own.

Further in we saw the oil rigs, and smack in the middle of a trap line was a pay telephone. In the middle of nowhere! In the Little Buffalo community, which has three hundred Cree people, there is not one pay telephone. Yet we could travel fifteen or twenty miles into the bush and, lo and behold, there was a pay telephone —unreal!

My major concern is what is happening to Native people individually and to Native organizations. When I talk about my people I try to bring their struggle to light. I talk about Native people as aboriginal people; I don't differentiate between status, non-status, Metis or treaty. There is too much at stake and too many people hurting.

"RELIGION ISN'T MEANT TO PUSH PEOPLE APART—RELIGION IS TO BRING PEOPLE TOGETHER!"

Harrel Davis

I'm Sioux and Choctaw. I grew up in Oklahoma, went to undergraduate school there and after four or five years, went on to seminary in Global, Kentucky. I graduated in 1981, was ordained and received my first call—not to the pastorate, but to the faculty of a theological seminary in the Twin Cities. In 1983 the Board of Directors of the Native American Theological Association (NATA) asked me to be the director, the first Native director in their five-year history.

NATA is an ecumenical consortium of graduate theological schools, denominational colleges, Indian training programs and lay training programs. The genesis of the consortium goes back to 1974, when the church first took account of the lack of ordained Native leaders in the church. A survey back then showed that of five hundred churches across the United States with predominantly Indian congregations, only sixty-eight pastors were Indian. And although they were ordained, very few of these pastors had had formal theological training. At the same time, in all the seminaries in North America, Canada included, there were only four Native students out of some 68,000. So that began the ecumenical discussions that led, in 1976, to the Native American Theological Association.

The association offers an alternative to the rather rigid four-year undergraduate and three-year grad-

Harrel Davis is a Presbyterian minister and the executive director of the Native American Theological Association in Minneapolis.

uate program that ministers normally follow. They began by pulling together every institution that involves theological education—not just the schools, but the denominations that respond to the students coming out of schools as well. At every point at which students encountered obstacles to their training, people were brought in who could speak to those barriers.

There are three ways a student can go through this curriculum. We call them tracks. Track One involves students who have a great deal of experience in the church doing pastoral kinds of things, but who have never been formally recognized. They tend to be in their middle thirties or so, and generally have at least two years of undergraduate schooling. In Track One they take the equivalent of the three year master's degree but more in depth and much faster. So after the equivalent of two years of college, then two years of courses, seminars, internships and graduate theological study, those persons end up with a university degree. People in Track Two are basically getting their education in the traditional way. They have their four year degree and then they're going on to seminary. The way we have an impact on their process is to introduce courses and experiences that are specifically oriented to the Indian community. Track Three assumes no formal education and has no requirements at all. The basic entry level is a high school diploma or equivalent education. These people take extension courses, seminars, internships, at least one year of residential graduate theological study and the balance is made up of other experiences. They receive a certificate of achievement. At least at this point in history, they have gone on to ordination with the various denominations under some sort of exceptional clause.

NATA is available in the following member institutions: Seabury Western Episcopal School in Evanston, Illinois; Dubuque Seminary (Presbyterian) in Dubuque, Iowa; Luther Northwestern Seminary (Lutheran) in St. Paul, Minnesota; and United Theological Seminary (now ecumenical, though with a historical tie to the United Church of Christ) in New Brighton, Minnesota. We also work with students at the Cook Christian Training School in Tempe, Arizona and the Dakota Leadership Program at Mob Ridge, South Dakota. Then there are a few colleges: Huron College in Huron, South Dakota and College of the Ozarks in Batesville, Arkansas.

The NATA process is oriented around three mission areas and one of them is advocacy. It is clear that we're working with systemic change. We're not coming to the institutions begging for an opportunity, we're coming offering to help the church. Leadership is only one way of doing that.

We are developing other areas now: a church-school curriculum, a journal for Native American theology. Parishes can certainly help by beginning to take up this dialogue themselves. The old question of the Christian religion having primacy over everybody else's experiences needs to be looked at. We need to see that there is something very valuable that Christians can learn from others—and that within these other expressions of religion there may be as much of Christ as in our own. It takes a great deal of courage to do that, but beginning the dialogue is the first thing.

My entire family are Southern Baptists from the Bible Belt and Southern Baptists they remain today. When I got to be around seventeen or eighteen years old I moved completely away from the church. It was convenient in those days to say: Well, I have to work this Sunday, so I'm not going to church. What I was really doing, though, was rebelling. It just wasn't for me.

It's by accident that I became a Presbyterian. When my wife was a senior in high school she was in a brand-new city, all alone in a very large high school. She soon met a person who was in exactly the same situation, who happened to be the daughter of a Presbyterian minister. They became fast friends. To keep a long story short, that minister married my wife and me and we kept our relationship up because of the friendship. Over the years I began to think of this person as representative of the Presbyterian theological outlook and I decided to give that a try. We had reached the point where we knew things were lacking in our lives. I had graduated from college, I had a decent job making good money, but we realized that the promises of education—the cars and the home in the suburbs—were not fulfilling our lives. When our seven-year-old daughter said she wanted to go to church, it made us look back at the old tradition and that's how we entered the Presbyterian Church.

Native American traditions were not a major factor in my life until very recently. My parents met at a boarding school and when they got married my mom followed my dad. Mother is a Sioux and is much closer to her cultural identity than my father was. His father was a white man. So the movement all along seemed to be getting away from an Indian identity. They moved to Oklahoma where the general culture supported their assimilation. I have very cherished memories of my grandmother on my mother's side coming to our home and speaking only in Sioux and holding me on her lap and teaching me little endearments in Sioux. But my cultural connection was not much more than those happy memories.

Midway through college, I began to think for myself about the issues of my life and I began to get very angry that I had been denied my right to be who I am. Then I began very forcefully to move back and try to reconstruct whatever I could of my Indian identity.

It's been a fascinating and powerful journey. I am beginning to allow that richness to have an impact on my life. I was a biology major in college, learning the scientific method, so I was radically opposed to mythology and all that business. I was skeptical of everything. Now I've been in Indian ceremonies. I have been in a pitch-black room where I've seen people sitting around the edges of the room, eagles flying in the room, and yet the room was as black as it could be—you couldn't see your hand in front of your face. And I have to deal with that. The power is real. It's unconscious, but it's as real as this table in front of me. And, this is starting to have an impact on my life.

I look at the Old Testament and the New Testament and see tribal ways, tribal situations. The people in the New Testament didn't have any trouble expecting miracles when they annointed the sick, and it went on regularly. The challenge is for us to go back and pick out the same things happening in the Native American traditional experience. I've been studying with a medicine man now for a couple of years—not really studying, but he's been helping me. He has explained things to me and what he says about religion is what I believe is the kernel of every religious experience: religion isn't to push people apart, religion is to bring people together. That's what I think lies in the future. We have to continue the dialogue. If we have courage enough to look at ourselves critically and accept others as important, then we'll move closer and closer to being together.

I think the future for American Indians is as bright as ever. The thing that Indian people have always had is their ability to adapt and in so doing, to survive. And that is going to go right on. A hundred years from now, Indians will be here. They may look entirely different, they'll be doing different things, but they'll be here.

WHERE HAS THIS NATION LED US?

The tale of Indians, I've heard it said,
Has been told in different shades of red,
From copper skins to blackened blood . . .
I've seen my people dragged through the mud.

Except for names carved into stone,
We are here, then we are gone.
The People fought honorably
As they were driven to the western sea . . .

Where has this nation led us?
We're here, then they forget us!
But all I want to be
Is set free.

Now my home has strange new scenery,
And as I search for my identity
Memories follow me everywhere,
It is sometimes more than I can bear.

I am not a savage pagan,
Wasn't born uncivilized, and I've never been
The kind of person who could stand the screams
That must haunt the whiteman in his dreams.

Where has this nation led us?
We're here, then they forget us!
But all I want to be
Is set free.

So I'll follow the paths my grandparents walked
As I try to speak the language they talked,
And try to be as best as I can . . .
A human being . . . A woman . . . An Indian . . .

Barbara Lavalley

*Barbara Lavalley is from the Seneca Nation of lower New York
State. She now lives in Canada.*

"THE CHURCH HAS SOME HISTORY FOR WHICH IT MUST REPENT."

Stan McKay

My home community is Koostatak on the Fisher River Reserve. It is 140 miles directly north of Winnipeg, along the big lake. Traditionally it's a fishing, hunting and trapping community. The population has been fairly stable for a number of years, around 800 people. There are 1200 to 1400 people on the band list but a lot of people are working elsewhere.

When I was a young child we had no access road, which meant that we were an isolated community. The nearest town was about twenty-five miles away by dirt trail and that was not always passable. When it was, we went by horse and wagon. But most of our travel was on water. We had more connections across the lake and down the lake than we had by any road system. It was very quiet, as I remember; there were very few radios in the community. We had coal-oil lamps, wood stoves, a very simple life. When I was about twelve, some thirty years ago, the roads came in. Gradually, the number of boats in the community began to decline and people began getting cars. The city and nearby towns became more accessible and life picked up five or six beats.

I was raised by my parents although my father, being a fisherman and a trapper, was away doing seasonal work for what seemed to me like nine out

Stan McKay is an ordained minister in the United Church of Canada.

of twelve months. So it was mainly my mother who raised me. We learned Native traditions and values largely through the way we lived.

For the first eight years of school I went to a small, two-room, Indian day school on the reservation. When I was in junior high I was sent to an Indian residential school about three hundred miles away from home. I didn't find it very helpful academically. After the ninth grade we were in an integrated program in the town, but the town wasn't very welcoming. There was, then, and I think there still is a fair amount of racism in that setting. So it wasn't a very positive experience.

I wanted to go to university but Indian Affairs decided that I wasn't capable of handling the academic burden. They suggested that I go to a teacher's college. So I took teacher's training and went to northern Manitoba to teach school. I taught for two years until I had saved enough money for three years of theological studies. Donna and I were married and I went back north again to teach. A year later I returned, completed my theology and was ordained in 1971. After twelve years in northern churches I was offered a contract coordinating Native work within the United Church of Canada.

I think the churches in North America have failed to deal creatively with Native spirituality. The imperialism, the colonialism of the initial mission onslaught into North America, the definition of Native people as pagan and uncivilized are still being applied by churches, sometimes in very direct ways. There is no understanding of who we are, of our heritage. We have to undo some of what the Christian churches have given us: for example, the sense that we bring nothing to the church; that there is no possibility of our ever bringing anything creative to Christian spirituality; the denial of our roots and our lifestyle if we are to be acceptable members of a predominantly white worshipping community.

Churches have not openly declared the racism of the western movies or the North American imagery of "savage natives." We have to admit that our racism *is* racism. I have been involved with some attempts to do this, though they are not very significant; they usually evoke a sense of guilt, then a liberal response for a time, but no real re-education happens. And as a Native person I admit that it also becomes racist when *I* began to define how the larger church should repent. I am not prepared to do that.

Within the Native community I try to affirm the spirituality and other good gifts they bring to the Christian community; that's my primary function. I don't sense a great calling to reform the whole non-

Native church. If what we do is significant and has some truth to it, then that in itself may give some vision to the rest of the church.

I'm learning, as time goes by, that yes, I have been part of the oppressive and non-creative elements that are within the church. But I think I have grown in understanding to the point where more and more of my work is directed towards helping people question and affirm the liberation movement within the Native community. I stress what we can learn from traditional spiritual leaders as we begin to see *their* truth. I am not totally clear on how this will eventually work out—I guess I'm on a personal pilgrimage at the moment. But I have begun to understand that the red flags theology professors used to wave at me came close to destroying the gospel for me. The only thing that the European invasion brought to North American peoples, basically, was the person of Jesus Christ. Anything else was an intrusion on the part of imperialism.

I am beginning to figure out that there *is* a Native Christian option. Very few people have considered it seriously, but that's what I am about at the moment. Native North Americans' wholistic approach: teachings about creation, the sustenance of mother earth, the interconnection of human and other life— these are aspects of the gospel that we have almost destroyed. Moreover, the oral traditions of the Native community preserve the biblical imagery of the Old Testament far more clearly than recent theological writings. Add to all this Native peoples' experiences of oppression, of powerlessness, of genocide, and this places us in a very unique relationship with the Creator. Our understanding of what we need to live and our spiritual strength go far beyond that of people who are trying to overpower and own the earth. As I say, I am still working through all this. And I am working with a lot more confidence than I had when I was studying theology. I am able to see clearly that all truth does not come out of the dogma of Europe— that there are other forms of truth that people have had for a long time. I think it is theologically correct to say that when one tradition or truth comes up against another, neither one is negated. In fact, both may have learnings to share.

My father taught me that the way to survive is to cooperate with people who are different, to accept the pilgrim and the stranger in your midst because that is the way you will learn and grow. He has a lot of integrity when he shows what the faith really is: accepting people with humility and dignity despite their differences. His introduction to Christianity came from Methodist teaching, but a lot of his faith followed from his own meditation and prayer life and daily faithfulness. He never had the opportunity for any formal education, nor were there many traditional spiritual people in our community—they had been erased by the missionary movement. My great-grandparents were quite strong medicine people but by the time I was little, only my great-grandfather was alive and he wouldn't practice anything in the open because the missionaries had forbidden it. So I only have faint memories of what some of it was like.

When the missionaries came into the communities, they became the religious authorities. They pronounced what was meant by heaven and hell and that gave them tremendous power. More than anything else, they brought medicines and claimed anything *we* had was less credible. They became the educators in schools, the judge and jury in disputes, and so on. And especially if they came with the sense that they were going to bring civilization to these pagan people they became very, very powerful. It was really my great-grandparents who suffered the greatest oppression.

I think that the church certainly has some history for which it must repent. There is so much said about profession of faith, so many pronouncements, so much accumulation of dogma and we print more and more material about our faith. But we have not confessed very much. And the inability of people to deal with the injustices in society from a Christian perspective is related to the fact that there isn't a way of being repentant. There isn't a way to really confess how the church has been involved in corporate activity which is genocidal, imperialistic and racist in its approach to minorities. There is a need for repentance, otherwise I think the Christian church will continue to respond out of guilt, momentarily, individualistically. And there will be no change of any significance.

I used the word "genocide" because I can perceive within society the ongoing process of the destruction of a people. No one can explain to me the tremendous Indian population in the prisons, the large number of Native young people in juvenile detention centers or the overwhelming number of tiny babies being removed from Native homes and put in non-Native foster homes or adopted. This trading and exploitation of Native children is, for me, the final step in the genocidal process. And it is going on in Canada. I have seen in the *Toronto Star* pictures of Native children being offered for adoption within the city. That really tears my insides because I know what is happening. I know of young people who as infants were adopted into homes in New Hampshire, California or New York, and who, when they reached fourteen or fifteen, suddenly decided they could not live in that environment. When they try to find their roots it is a very painful and soul-destroying experience. I compare it to Moses walking out into the yard of the palace, seeing the slave being beaten and being angry enough to kill the Egyptian. I think that is being replayed in society now; there are many young people who, like Moses, are filled with anger.

The church has to begin to listen to many people. The church has to evaluate the way it responds to Native spirituality. The church has to begin to look at its obsession with power and with the values and systems of society.

I have also seen that the church *can* be creative when it encounters difference. In the World Council of Churches I see some hope but I find there is little significant movement from the World Council level back into the local parish. The people back home tend to continue without any real encounters, without creativity. I am not a great visionary but I think people have to see themselves as prophetic. The whole question of how we heal the earth and the nuclear question have become so crucial in this modern age; we have to stand up in the face of these questions and make statements that are both concise and wholistic.

I am learning that we do not have to compromise. The Christian option within the Native understanding of the world is real. To pray in the four sacred directions is something I have learned to appreciate and statements in the Old Testament affirm it for me. I also find the use of sweetgrass or other incense in worship very significant. I'm learning how important the pipe may be. I know that singing, moving to music and dancing are very important. And the symbol of the circle is essential for any community that claims to be spiritually centered. None of these things require compromise.

At many points in this discussion I would rather have had one of the elders in my community speak. Still, I think the process of defining who we are is hopeful. There is a new movement, a questioning, and there will be an ongoing struggle. I think we are striking at the very heart of truth. There may still be a tremendous battle with groups like the Moral Majority because they perceive life quite differently than we do. We live in a period where the Christian community sometimes looks like a community of world-haters, and we have always been world-lovers. I tend to think the gospels are on our side—"for God so loved the world"—and we think we are part of that.

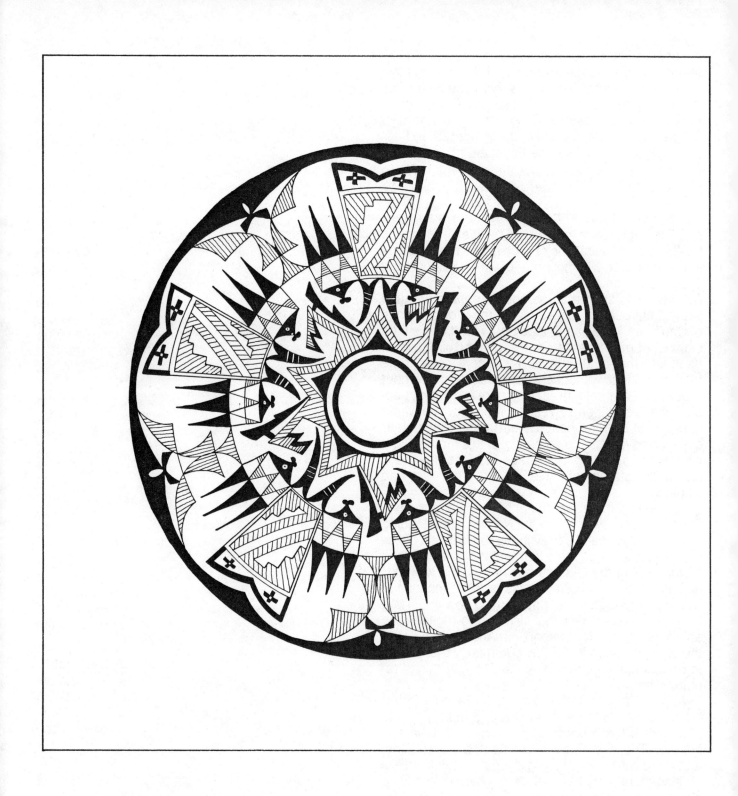

"HOW CAN WE REACH ACROSS THE FENCES?"

Tom Roughface

I'm from a community called White Eagle which is near Ponca City, Oklahoma. That's my tribe, Ponca. I was raised there. In Oklahoma we refer to our communities as reservations, but they really aren't reservations. At one time they were, but with the advent of statehood in 1906, just about all of our lands were sold. So we're governed by county, state and so forth. I think probably our community life when I was growing up was not much different than what people experienced on reservations. We were confined to our community by language and culture—and racism. I say that because we felt better by ourselves. We didn't fare well in the predominantly white towns. We felt more secure and at home among ourselves.

As I look over my childhood I realize that when you're very young you're not able to say, They shouldn't be treating me this way! Going to the public schools was a negative experience. I had to prove that an Indian could do as well as anybody else. I did pretty well and was able to get a scholarship to come to Oklahoma City University. In 1954 I was licensed to preach in the Methodist church. I got married in 1958 to a Chippewa lady. We're still together. Six children, eight grandchildren.

In 1959, we took a church with what is now the Oklahoma Indian Missionary Conference. This is primarily a Native American conference, an arm of the United Methodist Church—110 churches. A lot of very encouraging changes have come about since then. When I first came into this work, we were governed by a resident bishop and, at that time, the Board of Missions—now the Board of Ministries. We are now a missionary conference. We have the same rights, duties and privileges that the regular conference does.

The first church I served was among the Pawnee tribe. We were there two years and had a terrific time. Then I served one year among the Cheyenne people and got a different view of Indian people. Once again, I got a first-hand look at what racism is all about. In 1962 I came here to Oklahoma City and pastored what is called the Angie Smith Memorial United Methodist Church. I was there four years. They were quite a different brood of people, from many different tribes. They were urbanized; a lot of them were professional people like teachers, who

Tom Roughface is Director of Ministry for the Oklahoma Indian Missionary Conference in Oklahoma City.

had gotten away from the rural communities and become educated—a real change from what I had known the previous three years. A lot of my education happened during those four years. After that, I was appointed as district superintendent and served a wide area in northern and northwestern Oklahoma and in Kansas. They located me in my own home community back in Ponca City. I stayed there for three years and supervised the work of the Cheyenne-Arapaho churches. Then I supervised the work of the churches of the Pawnee. There was a five hundred mile spread between one end of the district and the other. Then I became director of finance and promotion for the conference for three years and got a chance to attend meetings across the United Methodist Church. I could see how Native Americans from across the country were getting a little restless and frustrated. After three more years as a district superintendent, I decided to become a pastor again. In 1975 I was asked to pastor White Eagle's Methodist Church. I danced for thirty minutes, I was so overjoyed—I just couldn't believe I'd be pastoring my own people! And I was there for six years.

In 1980 I was elected to our conference board of eight ministers. At that time, they were looking very seriously at ministerial numbers and needs in ethnic churches across the church and had pretty well determined that Native Americans had a crisis in recruiting people to be ministers. Some churches were calling back retired ministers, some were using laypersons to conduct services. So in 1981, the conference established a program of enlistment to recruit and counsel those who were interested in a church career. I became director of enlistment and training and I think today we have two dozen students either in college or in seminary.

We have made great inroads as far as Native Americans participating in the overall decision-making of the church. We've managed to get a number of our people elected to our Board of Missions. That is important to us—to be visible, to say to the church: "We have something to contribute." We were concerned about getting the church's attention, and not just a dollar here and there. One thing that bothers me is the way people romanticize Native Americans. They picture us wearing buckskin and sitting on a horse. They need to know that communities exist, that people are still struggling and are not accepted in a lot of places. We appreciate the church's attempt to help people know more about us, but we kind of like standing up *beside* people!

We may have a voice as a Native American conference in the Methodist Church, but you could still have a church—a great big white Methodist church—that couldn't care less that a Native church exists ten miles away. They might send six thousand dollars to Africa, but they won't send six dollars down the road. That's a long-standing problem in the history of our communities. You can walk down a road now and you'll see a white man with a fifty thousand dollar tractor plowing the land that you know was your grandfather's. Of course the white man is thinking of how *he* got that land. "We want to be Christian," they think, so (to massage their conscience), "We'll do something that makes us feel good." But they won't do something good for the person right across the fence. Christianity breaks down in a relationship like that, when we don't reach the fence, when we act like nothing's happening. Then we've got *real* problems. And that's my message to the Oklahoma Conference. I told them at their annual conference that we're going to have to stop sipping tea and walking away and not seeing each other again for another year. We need to come down and say, "Look, how can we reach across the fences? How can we build gates?" We need to deal with each other honestly. We need to have more dialogue. We've got to get beyond "respect". I can "respect" you until the end of your days but I may never really appreciate who you are. There are a lot of Indian people who choose to be separate, of course, and we're not going to change them. But I think that, by and large, those who really understand Christianity will learn to appreciate each other. I don't mean I ever want to *be* a white man, or that you want to be Indian, but we can still be brothers.

For the last ten or fifteen years, Indian people have really been searching for their roots, going back to what is traditional. The evangelization of the American Indian sort of rooted out traditional customs. The white man's values were preached along with the gospel. In fact, the "gospel" was that you couldn't separate the white man's values from the gospel! God gave each people, each society, its own ways. No one has the right to deprive people of what they have long respected and loved.

There is a strong Native American Church in Oklahoma. At one time, part of their practice was banned and they sued under the Freedom of Religion article and gained the right to continue their practice. I will be assisting them on Thanksgiving Day in Oklahoma City where they sponser a Thanksgiving dinner every year for everybody. A lot of them are young, half my age—people who are picking up the idea that they do *want* to be Indian and they see this cult and really go for it. Of course we still have a lot of Indian people who are Christians and who look at the Native American Church and think, "Well, we shouldn't be doing that. That's not the way it was preached to us." So there is controversy and confrontation between Indians who believe one way and those who believe the other.

From 1985 to 1988, the Methodist Church has a missional priority: "Developing and Strengthening the Ethnic Minority Local Church: For Witness and Mission." This means more than just handing out money. It's supposed to help us not only develop our plans and our needs, but it's also to help us get more involved—so we're not only recipients, we're also contributors to the United Methodist Church. We've gotten on the board that coordinates this work so we can make sure that the church stays faithful to its purpose. It's meant not to assimiliate but to strengthen churches wherever they are—black or Asian or Hispanic or Native American—to help them preserve what they've got and get to be a strong part of the United Methodist Church.

UNTITLED

Our destiny as descendants
Of the original people of this land
Is not negotiable
With any governments
At any time
Or any place
In any way.

Our destiny, our inheritance, our rights
And our responsibilities as
Children of God
Come from the Great Mystery Himself
Not from any governments
However constituted.

We did not cross the Bering Strait
As the anthropologists say.
Our ancestors
Were put here by God
To be the caretakers of this land.
We were not put here on this earth
To steal the inheritance
Of the unborn.
Our covenant, our bond,
Can only be with our ancestors
Who kept faith with the Creator's original
    purpose
And with those still unborn
Who will come after us.

Therefore we have no right
To negotiate the destiny

Of ourselves or of our children
Who will come
To claim their inheritance
In their own time.

We cannot, and we will not
Negotiate the rights to our future
With captive state governments
Who speak and negotiate on behalf of
Transnational corporations.
We are not confused nor misled
About their real intentions.
We believe that there is enough
On God's earth for everyone's needs.

And we have no right to abdicate our
    responsibility
Or to negotiate the inheritance of God's children
To the greed
Of the multinational corporations.

They call it progress and development.
We call it death and destruction.

Our rights as human beings
Come from God not from governments.
And they are not negotiable.

Among those rights
Is the right to live unmolested
And in peace on a land base
That is adequate to meet the needs
Of ourselves and our families.

Art Soiomon

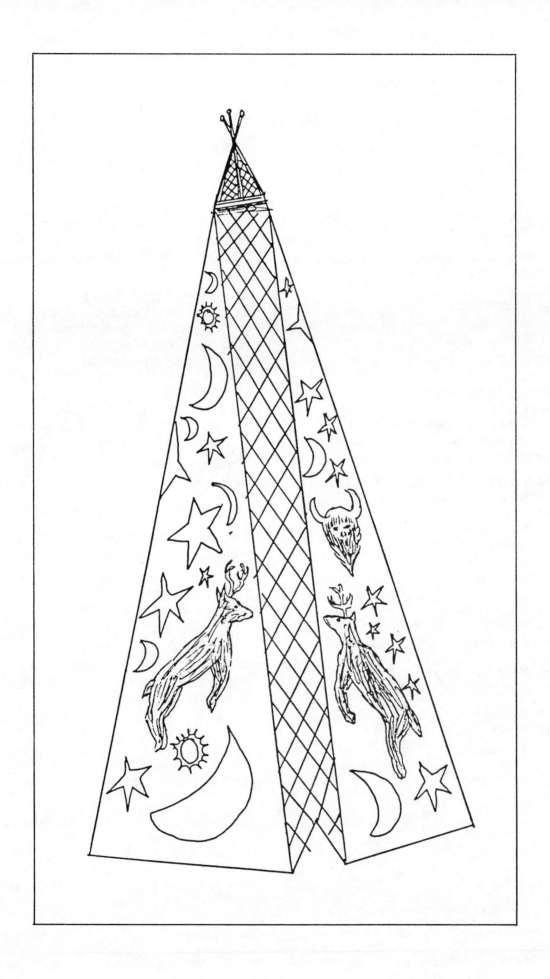

"I WANT TO USE THE GIFTS I WAS BORN WITH FOR THE GOOD OF OUR PEOPLE."

Charlene LaPointe

I was born and raised on the Rosebud Reservation in South Dakota. My mother and father are both full-blood Dakota Sioux. Until I was in the tenth grade, I mostly went to a Bureau of Indian Affairs boarding school. The matrons, or teachers, used discipline not to teach you something, but in a punishing kind of way. Today I realize a lot of them must have been rejects from the regular American educational system. They didn't like teaching Indian children, so they took their frustrations out on us.

In high school I found out about prejudice. I left school twice because of the prejudice. I ended up graduating in Buffalo, New York, of all places. You see, my father was an Episcopal priest and he had friends from all over the United States. One of his friends happened to be working on the reservation and he asked me, "If we got you away to a place where there was no prejudice against Indians, would you go back to school?" I said, "Sure." (If there was such a place!) That's how I ended up in Buffalo. But the prejudice there was even worse because the blacks would call me "honky" and "cracker" and whatever other names they call white people. And the white people would call me "nigger." They didn't know I was Indian—probably because I didn't have on the buckskin and beads and everything else.

After I graduated I attended Niagara Falls Community College for a while, but I was unhappy there so I left and hitchhiked all over the United States. I did volunteer work here and there to see how other people live. Then I finally settled back down on the reservation. I was going through a time in my life where it seemed to me that Indians didn't fit in anyplace. Schools were trying to change our self-image and our way of life, but we weren't totally accepted into the American way of life, either.

My field is in counselling. I've worked as a corrections counsellor in a state penitentiary and I've worked in the area of curriculum development for the American Indian Curriculum Development Program in North Dakota. Right now, I'm the director of a shelter for victims of abuse, mainly women and elderly people (we haven't had many men who were abused by their spouses). We don't work much with

Charlene LaPointe is director of the White Buffalo Calf Women's Shelter on the Rosebud Reservation in South Dakota.

children because the social services take care of that. The shelter is part of the White Buffalo Calf Women's Society. The society is incorporated through the state of South Dakota; we don't get tribal money or federal money or state money. We exist on donations from individuals, church groups and some foundations. When the society was incorporated in 1978, one of the areas of concern was family abuse on the reservation. In October of 1980, the shelter was set up. It's the first shelter of its kind established on any reservation. Since 1980 we've served, I would say, over fifteen hundred women and children and a handful of men. We provide short-term shelter for women who have run away from their husbands because they were drinking or something like that—so they won't get beaten up. We also provide long-term shelter for anywhere up to six months. We only have ten rooms, but our capacity is thirty-five. We have a 24-hour crisis line, we provide advocacy, we help the clients' families go to legal or social services or to court, whatever we can do.

On the Rosebud we have twenty Indian communities that are spread all over the reservation—that's 125 miles from east to west and 80 miles north to south. Some of the veterans who live out in the communities have expressed interest in working as intermediaries in situations of abuse. They could go out and take the man aside and at least stop it right there. We are also starting to work in the area of peer counselling, because a lot of women who have gotten away from an abusive situation understand exactly what other women are going through. There are a lot of shelters in the United States, of course, but the majority of people who come to ours are Indian women and if we have to refer them off the reservation, the counsellors in the other shelters might not understand the customs and traditions that Indian women live by.

I would say that one of the main issues facing Indians these days is water rights. Some tribes have signed treaties with the U.S. Government insuring them that they'll always have the water they need. Now we find that the government is trying to force all the different tribes to go to state courts to resolve the water rights issues. The problem there is that the state courts are, I would say, mainly controlled by corporations that are after the Indian-owned resources: uranium, water or land. So after the government signs the treaty insuring our rights to water or land, *they* are supposed to be the trustees of our lands. Just last October we had a meeting on water rights in Washington with people from the Justice Department and the Department of the Interior. One of the main issues we raised was that tribes do not want to go to state courts—they want to deal with the U.S. Government because we are sovereign nations within this nation. But the main man, the Secretary of the Interior, who was supposed to be at the meeting, didn't go.

Working here at the shelter I see people suffering from abuse, but there are contributing factors like alcoholism, which is one of the main health problems on this reservation. We also have to work in the area of education, because while most education teaches Indian people the American way of life, it doesn't answer children when they ask, "Why is there prejudice? Why don't people like us?"

I'm also involved in an organization called Women of All Red Nations (WARN). It's made up of women like myself who want to work on issues the tribal organizations can't work on because of the restrictions placed on money they get from the federal government. I'm active in the area of domestic abuse. The daughter of Thunder Hawk is active in a prison project she is trying to set up that would help families of prisoners travel the hundreds of miles to the penitentiary. As it is now, our people don't have much money so they get together to pay for gas and go all the way up there only to get to spend maybe one or two hours with the prisoner.

A lot of what keeps me strong today comes from the contact I had with my grandparents when I was young. That's how I learned the beliefs of our people. I was lucky that my grandparents were still alive when I was little. I've lost them all now. But my father was also very fluent in our language and he learned the values from his grandparents. He taught us that no matter how badly we were treated, we should always try to see the good in other people. It was very hard at the time, but as I get older I know that these are the values I am passing on to my son because they are what keep us strong.

I was raised as an Episcopalian but I tend more towards the Indian religion. It's more of a personal religion and sometimes the churches tend to force their views on people and it's really restricting. I was impressed when I heard that the Catholic Church had come out with a statement saying that when they work on Indian reservations they will reinforce the values of the tribes instead of forcing their beliefs on Indian people. I don't practice my religion through any one kind of ceremony, but mainly through the compassion I feel for other people. I guess the Christians propose the same view—you know, you put yourself last, you put your people first. There are a lot of problems within our tribes, so I have to be able to use whatever gifts I was born with for the good of our people.

CANADA

Indian
Section 2, subsection 1, of the Indian Act defines "Indian as a person who, pursuant to this act, is registered as an Indian or is entitled to be registered as an Indian. The conditions for entitlement are set out in Sections 11 and 12 of the Indian Act.

Indian Act
The Indian Act was an attempt on the part of the federal government of Canada to bring together and articulate the responsibilities it inherited from the British colonial government. The policy of the Indian Affairs Branch was embodied in the first Indian Act which was passed in 1876.

The act has been modified by various amendments over the years. The last major revision of the act occurred in 1951. Since 1969, there has been considerable discussion between the federal government and Indian bands and associations regarding further revisions to the act.

Indian band
A band is composed of Indian people of a specific group who are officially registered as members of that group. Although an Indian band is usually identified with specific reserve land, a significant percentage of Indian band members in Ontario do not live on the land reserved for their band.

Indigenous peoples
Tribal populations who are the original inhabitants of a particular region or environment and whose status is regulated wholly or partially by their own customs and traditions or by special laws or regulations, are known as indigenous peoples.

Inuit
The name "Inuit", meaning "the people", is preferred to "Eskimo" by these people. The Inuit are located mainly in Alaska, Greenland and northern Canada. The Inuit population of Canada is located almost totally in the Northwest Territories, Labrador, northern Manitoba and northern Quebec.

Metis
Historically, the term "Metis" was used to refer to people of mixed Indian and French ancestry. Today the term is used to include all people of mixed Indian and non-Indian ancestry. The Metis, not being legally classified as registered Indians, are excluded from the provisions of the Indian Act.

Native peoples
This is a term used to denote registered Indians, non-status Indians, Metis and Inuit collectively when there is no need to define the population boundaries explicitly. In other words, "Native" is a term used to describe the aboriginal people after the period of contact with the Europeans. Prior to the contact period, the aboriginal people were either Indian or Inuit.

Non-Status Indians
The term "non-status" refers to those persons who are Indian by birth, heritage and culture but who are not classified as "Indian" according to the definition in the Indian Act.

In 1874, when the federal government began registering Indians, many families and individuals could not be located; consequently, they were not registered as members of specific Indian bands. Some non-status Indians are descendants of the families that could not be located and also of those Indian people who were missed in the confusion or who boycotted the negotiations as a matter of principle.

Many non-status Indian peoples are Indians or descendants of Indians who once possessed Indian status. Some elected to forego their Indian status and become enfranchised. In addition, as stipulated in the Indian Act, Section 12(1) (b), an Indian woman who marries a non-Indian man is no longer "entitled to be registered" as a status Indian. As a consequence of this stipulation, many Indian women have been deprived of their Indian status and of potential Indian status for their children.

Reserve
Most Indian reserves are set out on land to which the Crown or federal government has title. The Indians have the right to occupy and use it; however, the ownership of the land remains with the federal or provincial government, depending on the way in which the reserve was created.

Status or registered Indians
"Status" Indians are those persons who are registered under, and subject to, the Indian Act. The majority of registered Indians are descendants of families that were registered by the Canadian government beginning in 1874. Other registered Indians are non-Indian women or descendants of non-Indian women who obtained Indian status through marriage to registered Indian men. As stipulated in the Indian Act, Section 11(1) (f), a non-Indian woman who marries a registered Indian man becomes herself a registered Indian. The children of such a marriage are also registered Indians. Moreover, the woman retains her Indian status even if she is divorced or widowed.

Specific claims

Specific claims are concerned with the administration of land and other assets under the Indian Act and with the fulfillment of Indian treaties. A specific claim is presented to the minister of Indian and Northern Affairs of Canada.

Comprehensive claims

A comprehensive claim, based on traditional use and occupancy of land, is accepted for negotiation when it can be shown that the Native title has not been dealt with by treaties or other means. Negotiations on such a claim involve lands, cash compensation, wildlife rights and other benefits, and may include self-government on a local basis. The settlement process includes participation in negotiations and settlements by provincial or territorial governments where their jurisdictions are involved.

UNITED STATES OF AMERICA

What is an Indian tribe?

"Tribe", among North American Indians, originally meant a body of persons bound together by blood ties who were socially, politically and religiously organized and who lived together, occupying a definite territory and speaking a common language or dialect.

With the relegation of Indians to reservations, the word "tribe" developed a number of different meanings. Today, it can be a distinct group within an Indian village or community, the entire community, a large number of communities, several different groups or villages speaking different languages but sharing a common government, or a widely scattered number of villages with a common language but no common government.

There are about 291 federally-recognized tribes in the United States. In addition, approximately 197 Alaskan village communities are served by the Bureau of Indian Affairs.

Who is an Indian?

There is no one federal or tribal definition that establishes a person's identity as Indian. Government agencies use different criteria for determining who is an Indian. Similarly, tribal groups have varying requirements for determining tribal membership.

Reservations

There are about 260 federal reservations in the United States. The largest of these, the Navajo Reservation, includes almost 16 million acres of land in Arizona, New Mexico and Utah; many of the smaller reservations are less than one thousand acres and others are less than one hundred acres. The Indian tribal government is the local governing authority on reservations, with the states having only those powers specifically given them by federal law.

Trust lands

A total of 52 million acres of land is held in trust by the United States for various Indian tribes and individuals. Though most trust land is reservation land, all reservation land is not trust land. The Secretary of the Interior functions on behalf of the United States as the trustee, with many of the more routine responsibilities delegated to Bureau of Indian Affairs officials.

Acknowledgment

Acknowledgment is the way to identify a relationship between governments. It means that it has been determined that a group of Indians exists as a unique political entity, that is, an Indian tribe. When the United States officially acknowledges that it has determined that a group exists as an Indian tribe, it means that as far as the federal government is concerned, that tribe has certain inherent rights and powers and is entitled by certain Congressional acts to other benefits and services.

Groups have been acknowledged to exist as tribes in a number of ways. In the past, treaties were one basis for establishing a legal relationship between tribes and the United States.

Have all groups been acknowledged?

Groups which never made war on the United States seldom needed to make treaties. Some groups claim to have treaties but did not seek (or for various reasons obscured by the passage of time were unable to obtain) acknowledgment. Some groups were so isolated nobody ever noticed them. Others chose to keep to themselves and avoid contact with the United States. During the period of the federal government's termination policy (1953–58), activity to acknowledge additional groups as tribes was suspended as the government sought to end its special relationship with Indian people.

Population

According to figures released by the U.S. Census Bureau, in 1980 there were 1,418,195 American Indians, Eskimos and Aleuts in the United States. This is a 71 percent increase over the 1970 recorded total of 827,268. The Census Bureau, however, attributed most of this increase to improved census-taking and the greater likelihood in 1980 that people would identify themselves in this category. According to the 1983 estimate of the Bureau of Indian Affairs, about 755,000 Indians live on or adjacent to Indian reservations.

INDIAN BANDS IN CANADA

Status Indian Population by Province
for Regions and Canada, December 31, 1978

REGION	NO. OF BANDS	POPULATION
Atlantic	29	11,389
Quebec	39	30,723
Ontario	116	67,460
Manitoba	58	44,642
Saskatchewan	68	46,275
Alberta	41	36,150
British Columbia	194	55,217
NWT	14	7,649
Yukon	16	3,244
CANADA	575	302,749

Source: Department of Indian Affairs and Northern Development

1980 UNITED STATES CENSUS COUNT OF AMERICAN INDIANS

According to 1980 reports issued by the Bureau of the Census there were in the United States 1,418,195 persons identified under the category American Indian, Eskimo and Aleut. This category, the Census Bureau said, includes persons who classified themselves as belonging to one of those racial categories and those persons who identified themselves as belonging to a specific Indian tribe. The Census Bureau's breakdown by states follows:

1.	California	201,311	26.	Idaho	10,521
2.	Oklahoma	169,464	27.	Pennsylvania	9,459
3.	Arizona	152,857	28.	Arkansas	9,411
4.	New Mexico	104,777	29.	Virginia	9,336
5.	North Carolina	64,635	30.	Nebraska	9,197
6.	Alaska	64,047	31.	New Jersey	8,394
7.	Washington	60,771	32.	Maryland	8,021
8.	South Dakota	45,101	33.	Indiana	7,835
9.	Texas	40,074	34.	Massachusetts	7,743
10.	Michigan	40,038	35.	Georgia	7,619
11.	New York	38,732	36.	Alabama	7,561
12.	Montana	37,270	37.	Wyoming	7,125
13.	Minnesota	35,026	38.	Mississippi	6,180
14.	Wisconsin	29,497	39.	South Carolina	5,758
15.	Oregon	27,309	40.	Iowa	5,453
16.	North Dakota	20,157	41.	Tennessee	5,103
17.	Florida	19,316	42.	Connecticut	4,533
18.	Utah	19,256	43.	Maine	4,087
19.	Colorado	18,059	44.	Kentucky	3,610
30.	Illinois	16,271	45.	Rhode Island	2,898
21.	Kansas	15,371	46.	Hawaii	2,778
22.	Nevada	13,304	47.	West Virginia	1,610
23.	Missouri	12,319	48.	New Hampshire	1,352
24.	Ohio	12,240	49.	Delaware	1,330
25.	Louisiana	12,064	50.	Vermont	984
				District of Columbia	1,031

NATIVE ORGANIZATIONS IN NORTH AMERICA

CANADA

Native Council of Canada
77 Metcalfe Street
Suite 200
Ottawa, Ontario K1P 5L6

Assembly of First Nations
222 Queen St.
5th Floor
Ottawa, Ontario K1P 5V9

Association for Native Development in the
   Performing and Visual Arts
27 Carlton Street
Suite 208
Toronto, Ontario M5B 1L2

National Association of Friendship Centres
200 Cooper Street
Suite 3
Ottawa, Ontario K2P 0G1

Inuit Tapirisat Canada
176 Gloucester Street
Ottawa, Ontario

Inuit Circumpular Conference
3900 Nuuk
Greenland
(Head Office) Or: C/O I.T.C.

Native Women's Association of Canada
225 Argyle St
Ottawa, Ontario K2P 2H4

UNITED STATES

National Congress of American Indians
1430 "K" Street NW
Suite 700,
Washington, D.C. 20005
Charles Trimble, Executive Director

National Tribal Chairman's Association
1701 Pennsylvania, NW
Suite 406
Washington, D.C. 20006

National Indian Youth Council
201 Hermosa, NE
Albuquerque, NM 87108
Gerald Wilkinson, Executive Director

Institute for the Development of Indian Law,
927 15th St., NW
Suite 612,
Washington, D.C. 20005
Kirk Kickingbird, Executive Director

Americans for Indian Opportunity
600 Second Street
NW Suite 403
Albuquerque, NM 87102
LaDonna Harris, President

National Coalition to Support Indian Treaties
710 North 43rd Street
Seattle, WA 98103

American Indian Historical Society and the Indian
   Historian Press
1451 Masonic Avenue
San Fransisco, CA 94117

Americans for Indian Opportunity
600 2nd. St. N.W., #403
Albuquerque, NM 87102

Arrow Inc.
1000 Connecticut Ave. NW
Suite 501
Washington, D.C. 20036

Association on American Indian Affairs, Inc.
432 Park Avenue South
New York, NY 10016

Institute for the Development of Indian Law
Suite 612
927 15th Street, N.W.
Washington, D.C. 20005

Native American Rights Fund
1506 Broadway
Boulder, CO 80303